ANGLING

— BRITAIN'S BEST —
COARSE, GAME AND SEA FISHING

1
West of England

2
South East and East Midlands

3
Wales and West Midlands

4
North of England

5
Central and South Scotland

6
North of Scotland

Individual waters, prefixed by their regional numbers, are listed in the Contents under four categories: Countryside Rivers; Lakeside; Seaside and Winter Sports – an easy way to help you to choose exactly the sport you crave.

A WORD OF THANKS

This edition published 1992 by the Promotional Reprint Company
Limited for Bookmart Limited, Desford Road, Enderby, Leicester, UK.

Printed and bound in Hong Kong.

ISBN 1 85648 042 9

JUST A WORD

BY ERIC MORECAMBE

Angling is the biggest participation sport in this country. It is estimated that there are three million anglers in Great Britain – and I'm happy to be one of them. Such a guide as this is invaluable for at a glance, readers can find the best places for coarse, game and sea fishing.

I've been a keen angler for many years, but in the hurly burly of weekly variety dates that punctuated the '50s and early '60s there was little time for a quiet spot of fishing. Nowadays I can plan my fishing activities with much more precision and I recommend such planning to readers. Frankly, I get a lot of fun out of preparing these expeditions; choosing my rods and tackle with care, plotting my destination, and knowing I'll be away from the telephone for a few days.

A lot of people find it difficult to understand the joys of the piscatorial art. They think it's boring, failing to realise that even if you are on your own there's a multitude of life teeming around you. A river is like a motorway, except that instead of vehicles rushing past there is a variety of wildlife constantly in view. And as an ornithologist, I get an extra bonus spotting all the birds that frequent the river banks.

Mind you, I've had my un-peaceful moments – like the time I fell in the river at Hampshire. I hooked myself while casting and overbalanced. When I emerged from the river, I was covered in slime. I had to completely undress and spread my clothes out to dry. Luckily, no one came by, but in case they did I should have told them that I was a nudist who had lost his way!

My favourite fishing haunt is the River Test in Hampshire, but I like the area once called Huntingdonshire and Carnforth, near my home town, where I used to fish for sea trout. Carp are my favourite catch, but they're tricky blighters. I usually bait with a fairly big crust, with a little piece of bread dangling on the lower float. This way the small fish nibble at the big crust while the bigger ones attack the smaller bait, thinking it has broken away from the crust. Which reminds me of the teacher who asked little Johnny, a keen angler, to explain 'the line of least resistance'. 'A fishing line without any bait on it,' answered Johnny.

But I can recall a funnier story – and this one is true! Some years ago in Blackpool I arranged to meet some friends for a fishing trip at six o'clock the next morning. I went to bed, set the alarm for five o'clock and, after what seemed hours I woke and dashed downstairs where I pulled on my waders and swallowed my cornflakes. But it was only two am.

I went back to bed, still wearing my waders, and slept soundly. When I awoke the sun was streaming in through the windows. It was a glorious morning for fishing, and so, now to meet my friends. Too late. It was 8.30am!

That's a real fisherman's tale – and a true one. But the real fishing stories of yore about 'the one that got away' sum up the true joy of angling and anglers who pit their patience and skills against nature.

CONTENTS
AND REGIONAL MAP

COUNTRYSIDE RIVERS

SEASIDE

LAKES

REGIONAL DIRECTORIES

WINTER SPORTS

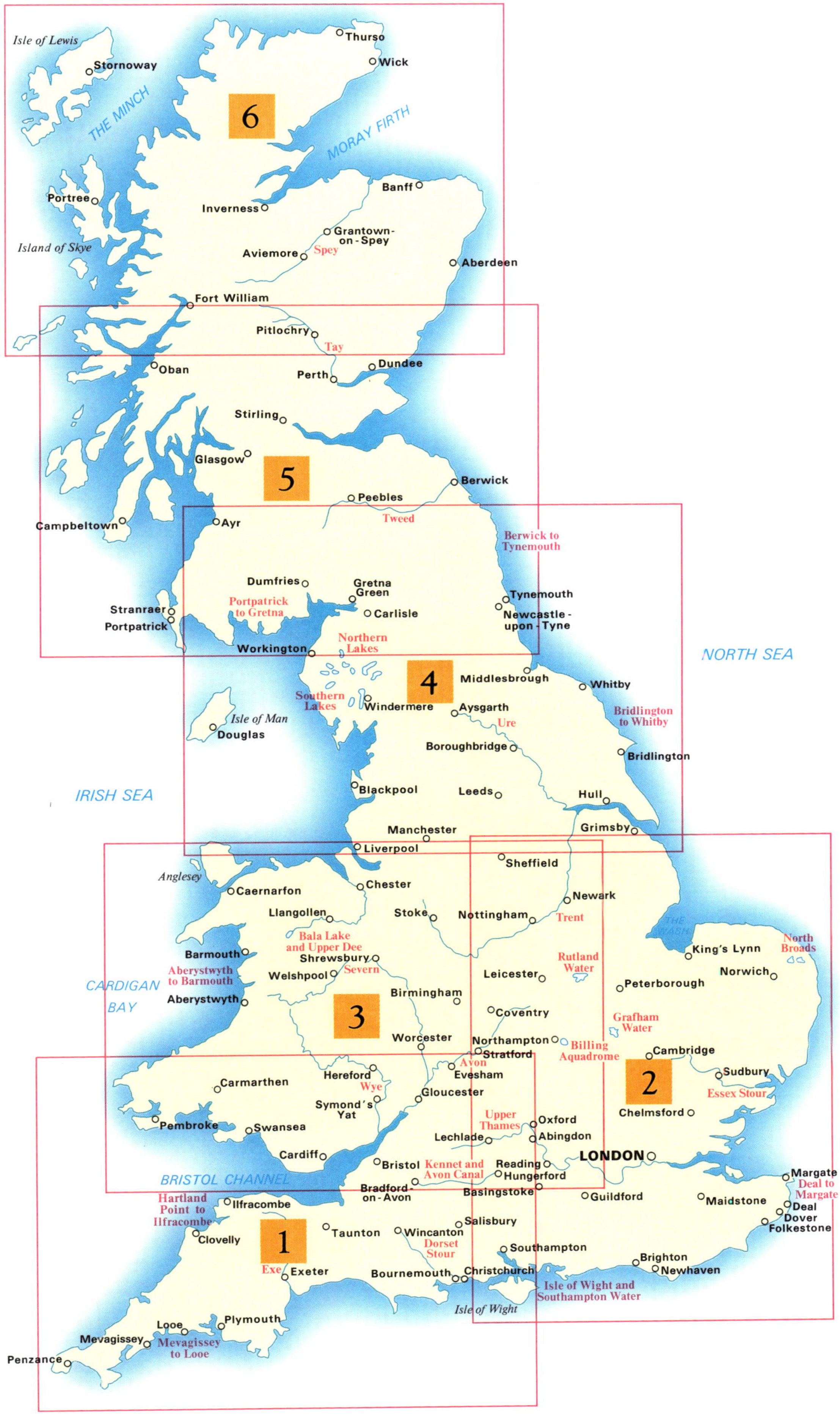
6
5
4
3
2
1
Isle of Lewis
Stornoway
Thurso
Wick
THE MINCH
MORAY FIRTH
Portree
Island of Skye
Banff
Inverness
Grantown-on-Spey
Aviemore
Spey
Aberdeen
Fort William
Pitlochry
Tay
Oban
Dundee
Perth
Stirling
Glasgow
Berwick
Peebles
Tweed
Campbeltown
Ayr
Berwick to Tynemouth
Dumfries
Gretna Green
Portpatrick to Gretna
Stranraer
Portpatrick
Carlisle
Tynemouth
Newcastle-upon-Tyne
Northern Lakes
Workington
NORTH SEA
Middlesbrough
Whitby
Southern Lakes
Windermere
Aysgarth
Bridlington to Whitby
Ure
Isle of Man
Douglas
Boroughbridge
Bridlington
IRISH SEA
Blackpool
Leeds
Hull
Manchester
Grimsby
Liverpool
Sheffield
Anglesey
Chester
Caernarfon
Newark
Llangollen
Stoke
Nottingham
Trent
THE WASH
Bala Lake and Upper Dee
King's Lynn
North Broads
Barmouth
Shrewsbury
Rutland Water
Aberystwyth to Barmouth
Severn
Welshpool
Leicester
Norwich
CARDIGAN BAY
Peterborough
Aberystwyth
Birmingham
Coventry
Grafham Water
Worcester
Northampton
Billing Aquadrome
Stratford
Cambridge
Avon
Carmarthen
Hereford
Evesham
Sudbury
Wye
Essex Stour
Gloucester
Symond's Yat
Chelmsford
Upper Thames
Oxford
Pembroke
Swansea
Lechlade
Abingdon
Cardiff
LONDON
Bristol
Kennet and Avon Canal
Reading
Hungerford
BRISTOL CHANNEL
Bradford-on-Avon
Basingstoke
Margate
Deal to Margate
Hartland Point to Ilfracombe
Ilfracombe
Guildford
Maidstone
Deal
Dover
Folkestone
Salisbury
Clovelly
Taunton
Wincanton
Dorset Stour
Southampton
Brighton
Exe
Exeter
Bournemouth
Christchurch
Newhaven
Isle of Wight and Southampton Water
Isle of Wight
Plymouth
Looe
Mevagissey
Mevagissey to Looe
Penzance

Location Map

Scale : 45 miles to 1 inch

Symbols used on location plans

- Motorway
- Motorway under construction
- Primary route
- 'A' road
- 'B' road
- Unclassified
- Road number
- Lakeside
- Countryside rivers
- Seaside
- Winter sports
- Priory, Abbey
- Windmill
- Castle
- Church
- Gardens, Parks
- Golf
- Manor, Museum, House, Hall

FIRTH OF FORTH
NORTH SEA
JURA
ISLAND OF ARRAN
FIRTH OF CLYDE
SOLWAY FIRTH
ISLE OF MAN
ANGLESEY
CAERNARFON BAY
CARDIGAN BAY
THE WASH
BRISTOL CHANNEL
ISLE OF WIGHT
Stirling
Greenock
GLASGOW
EDINBURGH
Berwick-upon-Tweed
Selkirk
Campbeltown
Ayr
Moffat
Dumfries
Stranraer
NEWCASTLE-UPON-TYNE
SUNDERLAND
Carlisle
Durham
Penrith
Workington
MIDDLESBROUGH
Kendal
Scarborough
Bridlington
York
BLACKPOOL
Preston
LEEDS
HULL
Grimsby
LIVERPOOL
MANCHESTER
SHEFFIELD
Holyhead
Colwyn Bay
Chester
Caernarfon
Lincoln
STOKE-ON-TRENT
NOTTINGHAM
DERBY
Dolgellau
King's Lynn
Great Yarmouth
Shrewsbury
LEICESTER
Peterborough
NORWICH
WOLVERHAMPTON
Aberystwyth
BIRMINGHAM
COVENTRY
NORTHAMPTON
Cambridge
Leominster
Stratford-upon-Avon
Worcester
IPSWICH
Fishguard
Hereford
Brecon
Luton
Carmarthen
Gloucester
Clacton-on-Sea
OXFORD
SWANSEA
Newport
SOUTHEND-ON-SEA
CARDIFF
BRISTOL
Bath
READING
LONDON
Ramsgate
Basingstoke
Maidstone
Guildford
Dover
Folkestone
Barnstaple
Taunton
Winchester
Bude
SOUTHAMPTON
Chichester
BRIGHTON
Hastings
EXETER
BOURNEMOUTH
PORTSMOUTH
Weymouth
Bodmin
PLYMOUTH
Truro
Penzance

TACKLE – WITH CARE!

Fishing is not a game of chance, despite what many non-anglers may believe. Like all other sports it cannot be played to the full with equipment which has not been properly maintained. Fate dictates that a cracked rod ring or a reel running dry of oil will not show until that really big fish takes your bait. Just a few minutes checking through your tackle before each outing could make all the difference between landing that specimen and rueing the one that got away. The guide, below, delves into the tackle box and highlights the techniques to care for equipment that not only land fish but also save you cash.

Baskets
Willow or cane baskets are expensive so it is worth keeping them firm and protected against wet rot. Scrub off all mud and débris, paying particular attention to the bottom and inside walls. Washing down causes the wicker to shrink slightly, tightening and stiffening up a sagging basket. After washing, allow to dry and apply a coat or two of clear varnish.

Disgorger
This small but vital part of any angler's tackle is easily lost – it sinks if dropped into the water. A small bottle cork drilled and pushed over the shank will float it – this will save you the cost of replacement.

Floats
After a few seasons most fishermen collect dozens – floats catch more anglers than fish! Keep yours in top condition by storing them in a foam-lined box. Check for cracked varnish and paint. The fluorescent tops will show up better if given an undercoat of matt white. Matt black bodies help to cut down fish-scaring flash during casting.

Flies
Watch out for rusting hooks. Flies are best stored in boxes lined with water-repellent ethafoam (foam rubber retains moisture and quickly promotes rust). Dry flies need treating with floatant spray before use.

Fly lines
These are expensive and easily damaged if not stored correctly. Run off the complete line from the reel and wipe it down with a soft cloth soaked in washing-up liquid. Dry it off and rewind it on to the reel. The nylon end of the leader should be watched for signs of damage and replaced, sooner rather than later.

Gaffs
These are dangerous if left lying around in the bottom of a tackle bag. Keep them safe by covering the point with a cork and give the whole metal head a light smearing of grease to ward off rust.

Groundbait
Finely-ground and dried breadcrumb is the best type of cereal groundbait. If kept dry it will last a full season, so store it in plastic bags away from moisture. For a good cloud effect, use brown crumb which has been dried in a hot oven to remove as much fat as possible. White crumb binds better and is best for fishing at long range since it is more clearly seen. It is probably better to add a little brown crumb for better results.

Holdalls
Protection for valuable rods is provided by a rod holdall. Never leave wet rod bags and an umbrella rolled up inside it – empty the holdall completely and hang it up to dry. Use an indelible felt-tip pen to write your name and address inside just in case it goes astray.

Hooks
They are the most important part of your tackle as they are the only items to come into direct contact with the fish. Keep them sharp during fishing by honing the points with a fine oilstone and keep them dry inside a plastic wallet. Small coarse-fishing hooks can be kept in photographic negative bags on which the size and line strength can be marked. Sea hooks and large coarse types need to be kept inside a waterproof box and given a thin covering of Vaseline to prevent rust.

Knots
These are best avoided wherever possible as they can be a weakness in otherwise sound tackle. If a knot is absolutely necessary, tie it carefully as nylon monofilament slips easily. Always use the correct knot for the job: bloodknots join lines of equal thickness; and a half bloodknot firmly attaches a hook. Never tie a knot on dry nylon as it tends to weaken with heat when pulled tight. Moisten the knot as it is pulled down and the join will be very much more secure.

A selection of freshwater hooks

A selection of spinners and spoons

Lead shot

Buy only the softest available – steer clear of the hard, black, shiny variety which can damage fine lines and proves difficult to remove. Look for perfectly round and evenly cut split shot. The best is usually a light grey colour and contains a high proportion of pure lead.

Each shot size is best kept separate for easy selection – 35mm film cans are useful containers.

Avoid sliding tightly pinched shot along the line or it will fray. A rough guide to shot equivalents is: one swan shot = 2AAA or 4BB; numbered sizes below BB start at No 1 (a little smaller than BB) and run down in size to Nos 12 and 13 (micro-dust).

Nylon line

The base material of modern line is nylon, usually monofilament. It is cheap and hard-wearing but strong sunlight will quickly rot it and reel spools should be kept inside a dark container when not in use. Check for fraying before every trip. Floating lines (used when fishing rivers with an upstream wind) need a light smear of Vaseline. For downstream winds, or when sinking a line for long distance work, wipe down the line with washing-up liquid to remove grease and break the surface tension of the water.

Nets

Both keepnets and landing nets should be hung up to dry after use. Store them in a plastic bag out of reach of mice. Nets with nylon content should be kept away from strong sunlight.

A fixed spool reel and a centre pin reel

A gaff in a safety cork and an assortment of floats

Reels

Centre pins, fixed spools and multipliers all need attention to keep them running smoothly. Wipe the outside clean before removing the casing to gain access to the gears. Once inside, look for any line that may have found its way around the main spindle. Wipe out dirt and thinly oil all moving parts. A special non-spreading reel oil is available at tackle shops.

Rods

Glass fibre, carbon-fibre or treasured cane fly rods need considerable care. Cane rods must never be left standing in a packed holdall. Dry it and hang the rod and its individual bag supported horizontally. If left in a holdall or propped in a corner they will take on a 'set'.

Carbon and glass blanks have done much to make rod care easy, but even these will benefit from a few moments attention. Check each ring for signs of wear and replace damaged ones immediately or it will fray the line. Keep ring whippings dry and ferrules clean and they will come to no harm. Cork handles will feel better if given a wipe down and an occasional gentle rub with fine glasspaper.

Sea reels

These must be protected from the corrosive action of salt and are best washed out in warm water, stripped and oiled after every trip. Sand can quickly cause serious wear if allowed to churn around for outing after outing. Bail arms need to be clean and free from dried-on groundbait if maximum efficiency is to be maintained.

Spinners and lures

Both sea and coarse lures need drying and lightly greasing after use. Check swivels for signs of corrosion and apply a smear of light oil. Hooks may need sharpening or replacing. Store them hooked in pieces of cork for safety.

Tackle boxes

Tackle will stay neat and tidy if packed sensibly in a good box. Remove dirt and grime for peak efficiency. Store leads in separate compartments to prevent damage to other tackle.

Umbrella

Simply open it after use and this vital shelter will last for many seasons without trouble. However after a time it may need re-proofing. Do this outdoors on a calm day by spraying with one of the special silicone preparations sold by tackle or camping dealers for nylon proofing.

Waders

Rubber perishes if left in the car boot for weeks on end. Wash waders down after use and hang them feet uppermost. Special wader-holders can be purchased, but a standard wire coat hanger can be pressed into service by slipping the wader feet between the wire and then pressing it to shape. Insoles will keep the angler's feet warm – but allow them to dry off after each trip. Newspaper, cut to shape and used in several thicknesses, will add to the insole insulation during cold weather.

Wire traces

Check for kinking and fraying – discard any that look suspect. Traces are best kept wound on spools or strips of cork away from moisture. Oiling postpones corrosion.

CATCH MORE FISH

Holiday fishing or weekend trips to new angling territories present chances to become acquainted with the many different species of fish, both inland and on the coast, extending your angling repertoire. In the guide to the main species, presented here, information is given about preferred habitats, tips are suggested to lure the species on to your line and targets you can aim for to get into the record books are supplied.

Coarse fishing

Barbel

This strong fish thrives in fast rivers such as the Severn and Hampshire Avon. It tends to feed over sand or gravel beds over which it patrols searching for food with its four whiskers or barbules. Barbel prefer a still bait and will take luncheon meat, maggots, casters or worms on a leger.

British record: 13lb 12oz

Bream

Found in lower (therefore, slower) river reaches and many still waters, the Bronze or Common Bream has a rather ungainly keeled shape and a small mouth. It is, however, a lusty feeder and considerable ground baiting is necessary to lure fish into a swim. Use grubs and bread baits.

British record: 13lb 8oz

Carp

This is the biggest of British freshwater fish and the one that has fired the specimen hunter's imagination for many years. Carp are shy and need to be fished with great cunning. Strong tackle is required and the angler must keep out of sight and be prepared to wait long periods for a bite – night fishing tends to bag the bigger fish. Carp feed at all levels and good baits are bread, potatoes, sweet-corn.

British record: 44lb

Chub

Almost as shy as the carp, the chub inhabits clean waters with overhanging bush and tree cover. Feeding at all levels, it is a greedy fish that will take big baits and it is predatory during the summer, feeding on fry. Most baits will be effective.

British record: 7lb 6oz

Eel

Small eels are sometimes a real pest to the serious angler. Over the pound mark, however, they become good sport and make a tasty meal. Eels spend much of their lives in freshwater but breed in the sea. Small dead fish or worms are bait.

British record: 11lb 2oz

Perch

Found in many rivers and lakes possibly encouraging more young anglers than any other species, young perch bite at almost any bait however it is presented. Gaudy stripes of older perch merge into water plant fronds and they exhibit considerable cunning. Small live or dead baits are used, but grubs, worms and maggots are effective.

British record: 4lb 12oz

A gravel pit perch

A fine tench

A trio of roach

Pike

Often thought of as the freshwater equivalent of the shark, the pike has powerful jaws spelling sudden death to any fish that strays within range. Pike tend to lay in wait for prey rather than pursue fish over long distances. It lives in most waters supporting fish stocks and the larger specimens are generally found in deep, quiet pools away from the main current. All forms of fish baits produce results.

British record: 40lb

Roach

Among the most widespread of all British species is the small roach. Enthusiasts can go a lifetime without catching a two-pounder but the delicately-coloured silver flanks and red fins of a one-pound roach makes a specimen fish in many waters. Fine tackle and precise techniques work best in search of this timid fish. Keep hooks small and lines as light as possible. Hemp seed and tares account for the largest roach in summer, but morsels like casters will take autumn fish.

British record: 4lb 1oz

Tench

Found in sluggish or still waters, the tench is most active in summer and is known as one of the hardest fighters for its size. Tench browse around lily and other plant roots feeding on worms and grubs. A strong line with worm or bread bait cast near to the thickest weeds will search them out. Bites are often slow to develop as the fish toys with the bait before deciding it is fit to eat. Coloured a beautiful olive green to gold, the tench has a finely scaled body and small red eyes.

British record: 10lb 1oz

Zander

An introduction to British waters from Eastern Europe, the zander is sometimes referred to as the pike-perch as it has some features of both fish (it is not in fact related to either). This is a predatory fish which is very rapidly establishing itself in East Anglian rivers. Fish it by pike techniques and medium-sized spinning lures.

British record: 17lb 4oz

Sea Angling

Bass

This fine silver fish likes shallow sandy beaches and will occasionally come right inshore among the breakers. Often referred to as the Sea Perch, it has similar spikes on the dorsal fin and it is a great sporting fish. Bass occur all round Britain's coast but southern beaches are a favourite haunt. Casting sand-eel bait into the surf will often find the best fish – ragworm is also a good bait.

British records:
shore 18lb 2oz; boat 18lb 6oz

Cod

Widespread in British waters, cod provide excellent fishing, especially in winter when the shoals move closer inshore. The cod is a scavenger that feeds on fish and worms – or practically anything small enough to enter its large mouth. Beach anglers should normally use lug or ragworm, but flashier lures and pirks are effective from boats.

British records:
shore 44lb 8oz; boat 53lb

A true bream

A common carp

Lambourne barbel

Kennet barbel

A freshwater eel

Conger eel

This pugnacious species is a real tackle-breaker and does not consider itself beaten even when hauled on board a boat after fighting every inch from the bottom. Conger favour wrecks, where they can lurk to feed on both live and dead fish which are the recognised baits. Strong tackle and a tough wire trace thick enough to withstand the conger's vice-like jaws and sharp teeth are essential. When boated, keep well clear of its mouth until the fish has been clubbed into submission.

British records:
shore 67lb 1oz; boat 109lb 6oz

Dogfish

Of the three species, the lesser spotted dogfish is of the greatest interest to the sea angler. Since lesser spotted dogfish hunt in packs, large numbers can be taken in quick succession. Keep the bait offered small – strips of mackerel or herring are best – on a single hook trace. There are a number of common names for this fish, but at the fryer's it is known as rock salmon, partly due to the pinkness of the meat. Do not gaff the fish on board if you can avoid it, as the species bleeds badly.

British records:
shore 4lb 8oz; boat 4lb 2oz

Halibut

Among the largest of all flatfish, the halibut is a valuable species which prefers the colder waters of the northern coasts and is found from 20–60 fathoms deep except during spawning, when it moves off the continental shelf to depths of up to 500 fathoms (winter months). Strong currents and rough sea beds are the fish's favourite feeding areas, where it eats almost anything that swims, including squid and prawns. Methods which imitate a sick or injured fish of up to 1lb weight on tackle of at least 50lb strength are effective. A large pirk kept moving from a boat will also take halibut. Commercial fishers have taken halibut of over 1000lb weight, so the record could be improved on!

British records:
shore 14lb; boat 234lb

Ling

A lover of wrecks, the ling is found over the same sites as the conger and is usually caught by boat anglers in quite deep water. This member of the cod family takes strips of mackerel and as it is a large fish with powerful jaws, tackle needs to be to the same standard as for conger.

British records:
shore 15lb 6oz; boat 57lb 2½oz

Mackerel

This small fish can provide good sport if it is fished for with finer tackle – a freshwater carp rod and 6lb line bring out the best qualities of the fast-swimming species. Small fish strips or a team of feathers can take mackerel in quantity, especially in the warmer south coast waters. It is a superb flavoursome fish when smoked or prepared by any method that will ameliorate its very oily texture.

British records:
shore 4lb 0½oz; boat 5lb 6½oz

Mullet

There are four distinct species of mullet of which the thick-lipped grey mullet (*Chelon labrosus*) is the largest and of the most interest to anglers. This is a very shy fish that will not tolerate thick lines and clumsy presentation of baits. Mullet can often be seen browsing around pier and harbour piles where they can be caught with bread flake or tiny ragworm pieces fished on fine tackle – number 8–14 hooks and maximum 5lb line.

British records:
shore 14lb 2¾oz; boat 10lb 1oz

Plaice

This very eatable flat fish with the delicately spotted skin inhabits sandy-bottomed areas coming quite close inshore. Shellfish make up a large part of the plaice's diet, but anglers take good catches with lugworm or ragworm streamed an inch or so behind a small fluttering spoon. This attracts the fish's attention and encourages it to lunge for the bait.

British records:
shore 8lb 1¼oz; boat 10lb 3½oz

Game fishing

Brown and Sea trout

These favourites of the game fisherman are widely distributed in fast-flowing and clean rivers and streams. The migratory form of this native species spends some time at sea becoming a silvery colour instead of the familiar mottled brown. Brown trout do, however, thrive in land-locked reservoirs where much of today's fly fishing takes place. Body colour varies considerably both with age and habitat – bellies are usually yellowed, changing to brown over the back. The characteristic spots end at the base of the tail. Trout are fished with both nymph and lure tactics, but generally deep-trolled lures take the larger fish.

British record: 19lb 9¼oz

Grayling

Clean, fast-flowing rivers and streams – ideal trout territory – are also the haunt of grayling. While not growing so large as trout (up to 4lb is a good fish) they do have a reputation as a fighter and can use their very large dorsal fin to harness the current in trying to break free. Grayling can be taken on wet flies and worms trotted into the swim.

British record: no record set – specimens over 2lb considered

Rainbow trout

This North American fish has revolutionised trout fishing in Britain. While some purists consider it second-rate compared to the brown trout, a rainbow is a spectacular fighter that characteristically leaps clear of the water when hooked. Most stocked reservoirs have large populations of this fast-growing species which is easily reared in stock ponds and trout farms. Like brown trout, they take both nymph and lure. Start the season with small black lures switching to nymph imitators later in the season.

British record: 19lb 8oz

Salmon

The King of the game river, this powerful and tasty fish fires all anglers' imaginations. Spending much of its life in the sea (principally in the North Atlantic) it runs up certain rivers to spawn. It is no easy catch and many experts believe that salmon take a bait only out of instinct rather than as a food. Once hooked, the salmon takes off at a furious pace and unless the angler can head off its first rush, there is little chance of a landing. Fished for with fly, spinner, prawn and, occasionally, worm, catching just one good specimen could cover the rather expensive day or weekly rod fees.

British record: 64lb

A large grayling

West of England

1

Cornish Coast

Looe–Mevagissey

Angling Associations
Liskeard & District Angling Club
Looe Sea Angling Association
Lostwithiel Fishing Association
Mevagissey Sea Angling Club
Shark Angling Club of Great Britain

Tackle Dealers
Jack Bray, The Quay, Looe
Frank Hoskin (Shark fishing agent)
Mevagissey Shark Angling Centre, West Wharf, Mevagissey
Tackle Box, Fore Street, Mevagissey
The Tackle Shop, East Looe Quay

HM Coastguard
Gorran Haven: *Tel: (072 684) 3429*
Mevagissey: *Tel: (072 684) 3332*
Polruan: *Tel: (072 687) 228*

Inland Fishing Water Authority
South West Water Authority
Tel: Exeter (0392) 31666

It is difficult to find any part of the Cornish coast that is not good for sea angling. The southern half of this peninsula has waters which are generally less exposed than those of the Atlantic coast – although nowhere around here should the sea be underestimated. The towering heights of the cliffs towards Land's End have brought about another branch of the sport, a combination of rock-climbing and sea angling, but in the prime holiday locations scattered along the coast from Looe to Mevagissey there is no need to go to such lengths for good sport.

An obvious deterrent is that you will inevitably be one of the touring millions who invade the West Country during the summer. You can compensate for this by judicious timing of your fishing excursions. Mix sea angling with a little game sport on the small rivers of the area and a fisherman's holiday could be a complete experience.

Counted among Britain's major sea angling centres is the town of Looe – or more correctly the twin settlements of East Looe and West Looe. Here is a thriving commercial fishing industry, often in the news for the bitter disputes arising with foreign vessels, methods and crews. Dozens of large and small boats using lines, drift-nets and trawls use the harbour, providing an unlimited source of interest to the visitor. Good water depth and an abundance of food here make bass, mullet and pollack likely catches from the pier. To the east, notably around Millendreath, flatfish are a principal target and to the west, at Hannafore, conger and wrasse are regular catches for those who are prepared to spend the time and trouble.

Looe's greatest claim to fame is as *the* centre for shark-fishing. Since the British Shark Angling Club was tentatively formed here in 1953 it has gone from strength to strength. Whether you are buying or hiring tackle to participate in this he-man sport, bear in mind that charter boats are in high demand and you should book a trip as far in advance as possible.

By June, blue sharks start to appear some twelve miles offshore and they remain until October. Mako and porbeagle movements are more erratic. However there has unquestionably been a drift of the porbeagle from more easterly grounds over the last ten years and sport is becoming more consistent. It is a challenging variety of sea angling

Big thirty-foot charter boats taking three or four rods at a time make regular summertime sorties from Looe. Trailing sacks of 'rubby-dubby' (ground fish and cereals) to lure the shark from the depths to the trolled or drifting baited lines, the boats ply over the shark grounds. A drift line may have a number of baited hooks on it at varying depths, supplemented by bait-only lines to draw the shark into the killing zone. These must be withdrawn at the first show of a shark so that it will take the hooked baits suspended from cork floats within thirty yards or so of the boat. Typical baits used are the oilier species of fish such as mackerel and fresh squid. Few committed sea anglers will be able to resist this breathtaking and challenging sport.

If you do find this activity a little too adventurous, and the family would like to get involved, go and see sharks (and many other fish species) among the marine collection at the Looe Aquarium!

Looe's local river is also split into east and

A fine catch of pollack

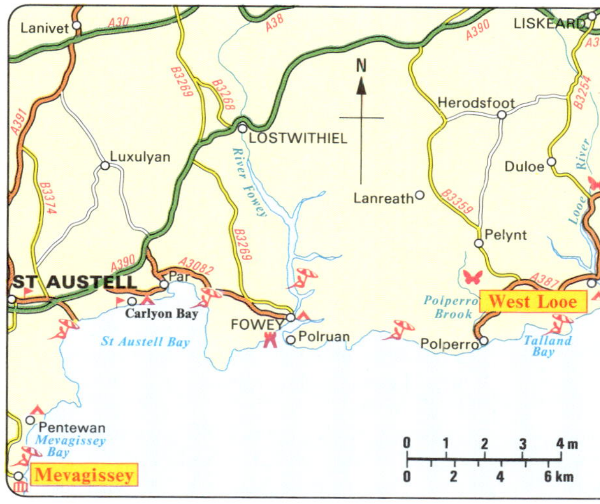

River Fowey
Excellent sea trout fishing Apr–May
Free fishing from Lostwithiel to sea
Water Authority: SWWA, 3–5 Barnfield Road, Exeter
Tel: (0392) 31666

River Looe
Fair brown and sea trout
Daily tickets: Botterell's, 6 Fore Street, Liskeard or Liskeard and District Angling Club, B G Wilson, The Bruff, Callington
Water Authority: as River Fowey

Polperro Brook
6-mile Cornish stream offering small trout
Free fishing
Water Authority: as River Fowey

west branches. Both offer good trout fishing with July as the peak month for sea trout. Consult local tackle shops and hotels for visitors' access. Towards Liskeard is the regularly re-stocked Siblyback Lake, a trout fishery yielding over 6 000 smallish fish in a season – tickets are available from the resident warden.

Only eight miles from Looe, past Talland Bay (which has several wreck marks of interest to conger specialists) is the lime-washed tourist attraction of Polperro – a cluster of cottages huddled round a picturesque harbour. Angling from the pier can yield bass, bream, cod, skate and pollack, with the best catches taken late in the holiday season. There are boats for hire here and you could have good fun with mackerel – always take local advice on when the fish are around as this fish is becoming a lot scarcer. A locally preferred bait for many sea species is pilchard, once a major catch in the area and exported in thousands of tons to Italy and the West Indies. Now the pilchard has almost completely disappeared from these parts.

Beyond Polruan, Fowey Harbour opens up and it is a prime spot for bass. The jetty itself is not a suitable spot as in common with many parts of St Austell Bay, around the headland, it has been polluted by china clay. The River Fowey's long estuary reaches almost to Lostwithiel and along the whole of this stretch you can fish free for salmon and sea trout with prawn as a most effective bait. Lostwithiel attracts quite a few game fishermen, since the trout here are good and in reaches above the town weekly tickets are available to visitors.

In the expanse of St Austell Bay there are one or two marks that have escaped the worst choking affects of the china clay mine run-off. At Par Sands and the neighbouring Carlyon Bay (below the beautiful cliff-top golf course) beach-casting can give good results. Angling improves immensely as the coast winds further south to the rock-and-beach fishing haunts between Pentewan and Mevagissey. The latter is an old world fishing village, thronging with tourists in the high-season. It has an off-shoot of the Looe shark-fishing organisation and several boats operate from here. While around the pier and shores fishing opportunities are limited, the bass are splendid. Boats also operate from here around the marks off Dodman Point and in the occasional mackerel shoals. Some very big mackerel are taken as are conger, pollack and turbot.

If you can penetrate Mevagissey in the season there are a number of family attractions in the village to be enjoyed. These include an unusually detailed model railway track layout complete with rural scenery and cottages for the devotee to study and a Cornish Folk Museum to browse around. For walkers there is the almost complete freedom of the cliff-tops from Mevagissey through to Plymouth which include extensive National Trust holdings. Other major activities which can be enjoyed by visitors are sailing (visitors are welcome at most of the clubs and one-week courses are available at Fowey River Sailing School) and golf. In addition to the Carlyon Bay Hotel course there is an excellent links at St Austell designed by the legendary Scottish course architect James Braid.

It almost goes without saying that the high-season temperature and sunshine and the many small beaches of this coast will guarantee that families on holiday will have few worries about daytime boredom. That this happens to be a stretch with better than average sea angling potential and several interesting game fishing rivers some fathers may not care to stress when suggesting the holiday to their family.

Camping
Carlyon Bay: Bethesda Camping Site ►
Tel: (072 681) 2735
Sloping 200-pitch (50 caravans) grass site
Open Apr–Sep, must book Jul–Aug
Fowey: Penhale Camping & Caravanning Park ►
Tel: (072 683) 3425
Grassy 56-pitch site
Open Apr–Oct, must book
Looe: 'Treble B' Holiday Centre ►►►►
Tel: (050 36) 2425
Mainly level, 450-pitch site
Open mid-May–Sep, must book
Pentewan: Penhaven Tourist Park ►►►
Tel: (072 684) 3687
Flat 105-pitch site
Open Easter–Oct, must book Jul–Aug

Golfing
Carlyon Bay:
Tel: (072 681) 4250
Clifftop course with superb views, 18 holes, 6501yds, par 72, SSS71
St Austell:
Tel: (0726) 2649
Well-bunkered moorland course, 18 holes, 5451yds, par 66, SSS67

Riding
Porth Hall Riding Centre, Sticker, St Austell
Tel: (0726) 4103

Sailing
Fowey River Sailing Centre, White Walls, North Street, Fowey
Tel: (072 683) 2318
Minimum 1 week sailing courses

General
Fowey: Castle Dore: Iron Age earthwork $2\frac{1}{2}$m N of Fowey, accessible all year
St Catherine's Castle: restored 16th-century stronghold
Open all year daily 9–dusk
Looe: Looe Aquarium: local marine collection & shark museum
Open Jun–Sep daily 10–6
Tel: (050 36) 2423
Mevagissey: Folk Museum: local crafts, mining, seafaring
Open Easter–Sep daily 10.30 onwards
Model Railway: fine layout including urban & rural areas
Open Jun–Sep
Polperro: Museum of Smuggling: fascinating look at smuggling history
Open Easter–mid-Oct daily 10–7

River Exe

Tiverton–Source

Water Authorities
South West Water Authority
Tel: (0392) 31666
Wessex Water Authority
Tel: (0272) 25462/25491

Angling Associations
Dulverton Angling Association
Tiverton Fly Fishing Club

Close Seasons
Brown trout: October 1 – March 14, *rainbow trout:* no close season, *salmon:* October 1 – February 13. Daily: June 1 – September 30: 8pm – mdnt, October 1 – May 31: 8pm – sunset

Bait
Trout: fly only, *salmon:* no shrimp or prawn permitted, worm and maggot only after June 1

Take an exceptionally good game fishing stretch, imagine the course curling its way through some of the most unspoiled countryside in England and you will realise why the upper River Exe is the West Country's angling Mecca. From the busy market town of Tiverton to the lofty tors and heights of Exmoor, the visitor can forget the hustle-bustle of the 20th-century and observe nature unchanged along the water's edge.

In Tiverton itself, many fine old buildings bear testimony to the fact that the town was once the prosperous hub of the South's lace-making industry. Tiverton Castle has more to offer the historian than the average fortress. A fine mediaeval gatehouse, fascinating clock museum and Joan of Arc gallery makes this Norman stronghold a must. Old Blundell's, a famous local school, had the author R D Blackmore as one of its pupils, the man whose *Lorna Doone* has given thousands their first insight into the wild and savagely magnificent Exmoor landscapes.

North of the town is Knightshayes Court. Those with a passion for rhododendrons should pay a visit to this country house with its fine array of shrubs. To the south east is the commencement of the Grand Western Canal, an intended branch of a system linking Bristol to the English Channel, which never materialised (much bric-à-brac of this ill-fated waterway can be viewed at the local museum). However, what *does* remain is a very pleasant towpath walk.

Ticket fishing for this region and up through the lovely Exe Valley is mainly via hotels. Brown trout and grayling are plentiful along this reach (as indeed they are along most of the upper Exe), whilst the bonus here for anglers is that there is no close season for rainbow trout.

Further upstream, some seven miles north of Tiverton, the river takes a sharp turn to the west, leaving the tiny Batherm tributary to flow through Bampton. In branching brooks such as these, rubber boots will suffice to keep the angler dryshod but in the clear mainstreams thigh length waders are the order of the day to stave off the torrents.

The quiet little town of Bampton comes to life in late October when many of the Exmoor ponies are rounded up and brought for sale at the famous annual fair.

At Dulverton Station, on the Devon/Somerset border, is the junction with the Barle, another fine salmon and trout river. There are many angling opportunities along this tributary and hotels offer the most likely access. In autumn the stretch of wooded valley from Hawkridge to Withypool is a stunning mass of golds and russets.

The first thing to catch your eye on entering Dulverton is the huge, and very old, sycamore that virtually obscures the ancient church tower. If you visit here during the summer and enjoy art, be sure to visit Exmoor House where local painters exhibit.

The town makes an ideal centre for anglers. The now-famous Exe Valley Fisheries consist of two large private lakes, re-stocked fortnightly, offering top class rainbow trout. In addition there is the 374-acre Wimbleball Lake, a reservoir opened in 1980 that is well-stocked with brown, tiger and rainbow trout. Picnic spots and walking trails fall within this very large

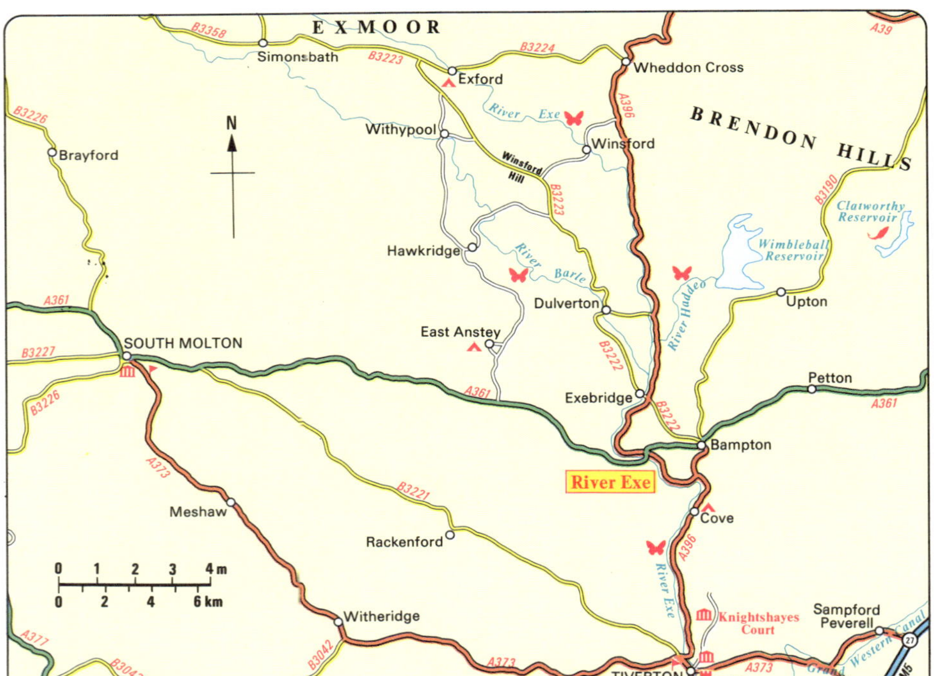

River Barle
Good salmon and trout fishing
Daily tickets: Lamp Hotel, Dulverton or Tarr Steps Hotel, Hawkridge
Water Authority: SWWA

Clatworthy Reservoir
Well-stocked stillwater 3m NW of Wiveliscombe
Daily tickets: on-site office
Water Authority: WWA

Exe Valley Fisheries (Dulverton)
Tel: (0398) 23328
Two lakes regularly re-stocked with sizeable rainbow trout
Daily tickets (in advance): Exe Valley Fishery, Exebridge
Water Authority: as River Barle

River Haddeo
Small Exe tributary offering trout and possible salmon
Daily tickets: Lamb Hotel, Dulverton
Water Authority: as River Barle

complex off the B3190 to Upton. Some six miles to the east of here, as the crow flies, is Clatworthy Reservoir. This regularly stocked stillwater has five miles of shoreline for avid trout anglers. As with virtually all the upper River Exe, the rule at these three centres is fly fishing only.

From Dulverton, the Exe accompanies the main Minehead road for several miles, splitting the Brendon Hills and Winsford Hill. Midway along this valley is Winsford, arguably the prettiest village in Exmoor. Six bridges, large and small, span the Exe within a quarter of a mile of the village green. On and up into the beautiful Exmoor Forest, the angler is dwarfed by moorland on all sides. With a glance to the right before reaching Exford, mist permitting, you should be able to spot Dunkery Beacon, the highest peak of the region.

Exford itself, at the heart of Exmoor National Park, offers many facilities to the sportsman. Besides fine stretches for salmon fishing the village is a centre for horse-riding, hunting and walking. As the best salmon runs on this section of the river tend to be from July to August, it might be an idea to plan your visit here to coincide with the Annual Horse Show, a spectacle held on the second Wednesday in August. The large hostel here welcomes ramblers and fishermen alike, whilst for campers the Westermill site offers simple riverside accommodation.

Beyond Exford the visitor cannot fail to be

Fishing the River Barle on Exmoor

overawed by the sheer stark beauty of the moorland, the honeysuckle and marsh orchids adding colour between the forbidding rocky crags, and the foxgloves standing like sentinels, thousands in a row. To the south of the river on a plateau some 1 300 feet above sea level is Simonsbath, an ideal base for both the Exe and the Barle. Here an old warder's house is a reminder of the days of forest law. Small herds of truly wild ponies and red deer may be encountered anywhere in this region and rare birds such as the kite, lapland bunting and great grey shrike also put in an occasional appearance. Indeed, the early evening angler may be lucky enough to spot the now-rare otter adopting his peculiar fishing strategy to catch the occasional eel.

Some two miles west of the B3223 Lynton road, high amongst The Chains, is the almost indiscernible source of the Exe, little more than two miles from that of the Barle.

South Molton and Lynton (alas, not a good sea fishing resort) are within striking distance of this elevated spot. Both these towns have informative museums for those wishing to delve deeper into the natural history and lore of Exmoor.

The cost of angling our selected thirty-two-mile stretch of river is a little high, but the marvellous environment amply compensates.

Camping
Cove: Orchard Caravan Park ►
Tel: (039 83) 563
Well-spaced 13-pitch site
Open Easter–Oct, must book
East Anstey: Zeacombe Caravan & Camping Park ►►►
Tel: (039 84) 279
Rural 40-pitch site
Open mid-May–mid-Nov, should book Jul–Aug
Exford: Westermill ►
Tel: (064 383) 238
60-pitch riverside site
Open late May–Oct, must book Jul–Aug

Golfing
South Molton: Bourne Bridge
Tel: (088 481) 394
Parkland course 7m SE of South Molton off A373, 18 holes, 5520yds, par 70
Tiverton:
Tel: (088 42) 2187
Meadowland course, 18 holes, 6193yds, par 71, SSS69

Walking Trails
Cloutsham Nature Trail: 3m ($1\frac{1}{2}$hr) circular woodland walk. Start from Webber's Post, 1m E of Exford off B3224
Grand Western Canal: pleasant 11m towpath walk starting at SE edge of Tiverton

General
Lynton: Lyn & Exmoor Museum: local history plus old Barnstaple railway relics
Open Apr–Sep (ex Sat) 10–5 (Sun 2–5)
South Molton: Castle Hill: 18th-century mansion with ornamental gardens, 4m W of South Molton off A361
Tiverton: Knightshayes Court: 19th-century house with varied flower gardens
Open Apr–Oct daily 12.30–6 (house 1.30–6)
Tiverton Castle: 12th-century stronghold with notable gatehouse
Open Easter then mid-May–mid-Sep daily 2.30–5.30 (ex Fri & Sat)
Tel: (088 42) 3200
Tiverton Museum: numerous local exhibits plus wartime, agricultural & railway sections
Open all year (ex Sun)
Tel: (088 42) 2446

North Devon Coast

Hartland Point – Ilfracombe

Angling Associations
Barnstaple and District Angling Association
Bideford and District Angling Association
Ilfracombe and District Angling Association

Tackle Dealers
Rod Room, 93 Boutport Street, Barnstaple
The Sports Centre, 139 High Street, Ilfracombe
E W G Stacey, 15 Bear Street, Barnstaple

HM Coastguard
Croyde: *Tel: (0271) 890329*
Hartland: *Tel: (023 74) 235*
Ilfracombe: *Tel: (0271) 62117*

Inland Fishing Water Authority
South West Water Authority
Tel: Exeter (0392) 31666

Stepped out into the sea in Britain's south west corner, the north coast of Devon bears the full brunt of the weather-driven rollers of the Atlantic. Rocks and cliffs rise to dramatic heights, there is a considerable water depth close inshore and this is in contrast to the sudden expanses of wide sandy beach, loved by surfers, that vent the coastline. This coast is probably the wildest and most beautiful in the whole of the county.

While it is true that angling on the stretch of coast from Hartland Point around the great bite of Barnstaple Bay to Ilfracombe is eclipsed by the excitement of the wreck fishing further south and the drama of the fight for shark out of Looe and Mevagissey, it is a fruitful surf-casting area and a prime holiday location. Waters are exceptionally clear, there is not the pressure on charter boat facilities and, compared to the wilder Cornish coast, much more inshore boat and surf-casting is possible.

Undoubtedly the most picturesque old port of the selected area is Clovelly, where residents and tourists can still totally disregard the car, banished from the steep cobblestone 'main' street. If the thought of walking daunts you, you can go by donkey. Festooned with the flowers from overhanging gardens the road leads down to the cliff's foot and the bluff stone quay of the busy harbour. Here, beside the lifeboat house, are several craft for hire. Waters around Clovelly yield bull huss, cod, conger, dogfish and some whiting all year round. As the porbeagle shark continues to show a tendency to head round Britain's western extremity, boats out of harbours in this area can strike towards Hartland Point. Off the vertigious cliffs, this shark has been caught in increasing numbers. Clovelly is not, however, a good base for the shore-bound angler, as the quay is closed during the summer and visitors pour into the environs in hordes.

From Clovelly harbour you may just be able to see a small cluster of cottages three miles to the east. It is the secluded resort of Buck's Mills which has very good beach-fishing, especially at low tide.

Further east, round Abbotsham Cliffs and across the comparatively sheltered Bideford Bay is Westward Ho! the oddly named holiday town and local golfing Mecca. Here there is an extensive sandy beach with good rock-fishing vantage points. Bass, dogfish and tope are likely catches.

Appledore guards the entrance to the double estuary of the Torridge and Taw rivers and it is today much as Charles Kingsley described it – 'the little white fishing village'. It has the rare amenity of a free boat park and many people bring dinghies down here for launch. Consequently it is a popular water ski-ing spot and beach casters should beware of the speeding boats. Nearby rock-fishing is good for bass, and the odd cod of 20lb or so has been taken here in winter. There is a salmon run in the estuary and these fish are taken commercially on a small scale. Several well-placed marks along the estuary offer most of the normal sea species.

Opposite Appledore are the firm safe beaches of Instow favoured by many local bass fishermen. This is an ideal place for the family as children can play safely around the dunes and bathing is equally worry-free. Instow quay, which can be reached by ferry from Appledore, is the home of the North Devon Yacht Club, who offer facilities for visitors.

Most parts of the estuary are reliable bets for mullet if you have the technique and finesse to

Camping
Clovelly: Steart Farm ►►►
Tel: (023 73) 239
Undulating 60-pitch site, 5m E of Clovelly off A39
Open Easter–Oct no bookings.
Croyde Bay: Ruda Holiday Park ►►►►
Tel: (0271) 890671
Gently-rolling 400-pitch site
Open Easter–Oct, must book Jul–Aug
Ilfracombe: Big Meadow Camping Site ►
Tel: (0271) 62282
150-pitch site near sea
Open May–Oct, no bookings
Woolacombe: Golden Coast Holiday Village ►►►►
Tel: (027 187) 418
231-pitch camping complex
Open Easter–Sep, must book

Golfing
Ilfracombe:
Tel: (0271) 62176
Clifftop course with fine views, 18 holes, 5823yds, par 69, SSS68
Saunton (Braunton):
Tel: (0271) 812436
Windy links course, 18 holes, 6675yds, par 70, SSS73
Westward Ho!:
Royal North Devon
Tel: (023 72) 3817
Windy seaside course, 18 holes, 6639yds, par 71, SSS72

Walking Trails
Cowley Cleave Nature Trail: ¾m (½hr) signposted woodland walk. Take turning to Parracombe 8m E of Ilfracombe off A399

General
Appledore: N Devon Maritime Museum: naval paintings, craft & models
Open Easter–Sep 2.30–5.30
Barnstaple:
Marwood Hill: 10 acres of rare trees, shrubs & gardens
Open all year
Tel: (0271) 2528
Bideford: Burton Art Gallery: modern collection of pictures & *objets d'art*
Open all year daily (ex Sun)
Tel: (023 72) 6711
Clovelly: beautiful village with cobblestone streets, unique in having no vehicular access. B3237, off A39, leads to car park
Ilfracombe:
Ilfracombe Museum: history, geology, Victoriana
Open daily 10–5 (10–1 winter)
Tel: (0271) 63541
Instow: Tapeley Park House & Gardens: Italianate garden, woodland walks, putting green
Open Easter–Oct 10–6 (ex Mon)
Tel: (0271) 860528

River Taw
Good game and coarse fishing with some chances for visitors
Free fishing from Week (4m S of Barnstaple) to sea
Water Authority: SWWA
Tel: (0392) 31666

River Torridge
Trout and salmon near estuary
Daily tickets (from riparian owner): C R Rowe, The Holt, Appledore, Devon
Tel: (023 72) 3126
Water Authority: as River Taw

River Yeo
Taw tributary offering trout and sea trout
Daily tickets (Mon–Fri only): Rod Room, 93 Boutport Street, Barnstaple, Devon
Water Authority: as River Taw

catch this most fastidious and hook-shy of sea fish. There are plenty of locally available rag and lugworm baits and you can also use bread paste – but never use any more than a 7lb line and a sliver of bait or the mullet shies off. While imitation sand-eels tend to take the biggest bass off these shores, beach-casting in the late evening or even into the night with rag, lug worm or soft crab takes impressive catches.

It is worth noting that, if you do like to mix your fishing, both the Torridge and the Taw are fine game rivers. Although dace and roach seem to infest the Taw, salmon and sea trout can be taken in good quantities on ticket stretches, controlled, in the main, by hotels. Day tickets are also available for fly-fishing trout on the Yeo, a Taw tributary and on the Torridge – enquire at local tackle shops.

Along the northern side of the Taw estuary, beyond the mouth of the tiny River Caen is the sandy waste of Braunton Burrows. Since 1964 it has been designated a National Nature Reserve and it abounds with wild flowers and rare sea birds. This is a coast that is particularly exposed to the incoming rollers and, at Croyde Bay and Woolacombe Sands (Morte Bay), the surfers have a fine time. Beach-casting is only viable in the evenings due to the crowds, but there are some stands around Baggy Point (which separates the two bays) where bass are extremely lively.

Beyond Morte Point the fishing is a different world. From here through to Ilfracombe the sea angling takes some beating. Sheer variety of species and a fairly accessible shore are big lures to anglers – the fish take worms, artificial baits and fish strip. That also goes for bass, cod, conger, grey whiting, pollack, pout whiting (locally known as glower), some skate and occasional tope. Mackerel have not been quite so good in recent years but they still offer sport in high summer, using trolled feathers. Vessels from Ilfracombe are very reliable and it must be emphasised that an experienced boatman is essential in these sometimes hostile waters.

Around the town itself there are good rock and beach stands at Hillsborough, Broadstrand beach and Hele Bay. The town pier can be fished, but no bait digging is allowed in the harbour during the summer months.

Again for a bit of variety, visitors are welcome to fish the Slade Reservoirs just outside Ilfracombe – tickets are sold on-site for this trout-stocked water.

This is a region that has many coastal campsites, often within a short walk of good fishing. Examples are the large, well-equipped Ruda Holiday Park site at Croyde Bay, and the Golden Coast site near Woolacombe.

Beaches, rock pools and the usual delights of the main resort towns will be the natural attractions to keep non-anglers, especially younger children, amused. Westward Ho! is not the only course in the area for golf fans either, although the Royal North Devon club is one of the oldest in Britain (founded in 1864). Saunton, an exposed course on the edge of Braunton Burrows, is a first class links and Ilfracombe has a fine course on the cliff tops. Active walkers have too many opportunities to mention but this section of the way-marked South West Coastal Path explores some very varied terrain.

When the weather is really rough and the fish retreat beyond casting range, you can go and see how the seafarers of old, fishermen, explorers and wreckers, coped with such conditions at the North Devon Maritime Museum in Appledore. The museum houses old craft, a collection of extremely detailed scale models and some fascinating reminders of the hard life many West Country men faced in making a living against the elements.

Fishing boats at Ilfracombe

Dorset Stour

Mudeford – Blandford Forum

Water Authority
Wessex Water Authority
Tel: (0272) 25462/25491

Angling Associations
Blandford & District Angling Association
Christchurch Angling Club
Durweston Angling Society
Southampton Piscatorial Society (2m at Sturminster Marshall)
Wimborne & District Angling Club

Close Seasons
Coarse fish: March 15 – June 15, *salmon:* October 1 – February 28, *sea trout:* November 1 – April 14, *brown & rainbow trout:* October 16 – March 31

Catch Records
Barbel: 13-14-0, *carp:* 10-11-0, *salmon:* 48-0-0, *trout:* 9-0-0

Although for many years overshadowed by, and derisively referred to as a tributary of the mighty River Avon, the Dorset Stour, as any discerning angler will hasten to tell you, is a very fine river in its own right. Indeed, the quality of coarse fish in the lower reaches bears comparison with that of any English river and offers endless hours of sport.

The Stour and the Avon share the same estuary which runs from the sea at Mudeford (where salmon run the gauntlet of the professional seine netters) to Christchurch Harbour. In these sheltered waters, mullet continues to be a prime species for sea anglers during the summer months.

Before the two rivers part company, but just beyond tidal limits, is the stretch owned by the West Hants Water Company, known as the Royalty Fishery. This centre is justly famed not only for its salmon and trout, but also many coarse fish, notably barbel. It is a curious irony that barbel were only introduced to the Avon and the Stour at the turn of the century by keen anglers from the Thames. Yet now, despite the obvious over-fishing problems which have beset Royalty and Throop (another fishery up-river), the Dorset and Hampshire rivers are still hard to match for this species. Certainly no other fishery can boast such a high sea trout catch. Permits here are occasionally available, but for obvious reasons very limited.

Whilst in the Christchurch region, if you are a fortress fiend, be sure to visit Christchurch Castle. These 11th-century ruins surround a rare example of a Norman house. On the outskirts of the town is the miniature world of Tucktonia, a large pleasure ground containing many British buildings, made to scale and skilfully animated. This comparatively new complex has already established itself as a firm tourist favourite.

Just along the coast is the ever-popular resort of Bournemouth, with plenty of interesting local attractions for the tourist. In and around the town centre are many notable exhibitions and galleries. However, if you are down near the pier (and not dangling a line for chub, garfish or sole!) and fancy browsing at something a little different, then try the British Typewriter Museum. Or, if walking is your thing, then Bournemouth has several elevated parks, notably Queen's, commanding delightful views of the New Forest.

Moving a little further up-river, at Holdenhurst is the five and a half-mile stretch known as Throop Fisheries. Another rated centre for anglers, Throop offers top quality barbel, chub and roach. Salmon runs here, however, have tended to decline in recent years, but most anglers will be more than pleased with the standard of trout. Short-term permit fishing is available for all species.

In this same area, the budding Jack Nicklaus has three golf clubs to choose from – Knighton Heath, as its name suggests, a pleasant heathland course; Ferndown, a pretty eighteen holes to the north, and Broadstone in scrubland south of Wimborne.

At Wimborne, a pleasant little town with major market-gardening and small industry, the focal point is the Minster. This Norman-to-15th-century church houses a chained library, an enormous c1320 clock and a rare vellum manuscript of the same era.

A little to the south of the town is Merley Bird Gardens, an Aladdin's cave for birdwatchers. Apart from several large aviaries there is mini-golf, pets corner and various novelty rides, making the three-acre complex a pleasant place for the family to while away a few hours. To the north, campers may like to earmark Wilksworth Farm Caravan Park for an agreeable overnight stay.

Roughly tracing the route from Merley to Wilksworth, the River Allen bisects Wimborne from south to north on its weaving course back to the source in the chalky uplands of Cranborne. Quality trout and coarse fish can be expected from this Stour tributary. Best access is through local hotels or, if you prefer boat-fishing, vessels can be hired from Canford Bridge. It should be borne in mind that day tickets for these waters are scarce, so book in advance or be prepared for disappointment.

Upstream past Corfe Mullen, is Sturminster Marshall where the Stour is crossed by an ancient bridge. This qualifies as one of the prettiest stretches of the river. From here, striking out north-eastward along a country road for some three miles, you will reach Badbury Rings. This Iron Age earthwork consists of three concentric circles of massive chalk trenches enclosing a copse. It is thought to have been the site of an Anglo-Saxon battle in the misty past. Back in Wimborne, further data can be gleaned at Priest's House Museum.

On approaching Blandford, ticket fishing is more readily available. Here the river is particularly good for chub, dace and roach. The Wessex Water Authority has recently added stocks of bream in the slower, deeper sections in this area as an experiment.

To show how seriously anglers of the past took their sport, within the boundary of Blandford on a bridge over the weed-dappled Stour, is a plaque bearing the whimsical caution – 'Anyone found "injuring" the river is liable to be transported for life'.

The mainly Georgian town of Blandford (or Blandford Forum to Latin scholars), used to be known for its stained glass, buttons and lace, but nowadays beer is by far the town's main product. The long-established army camp

Fishing at Lower Throop Fishery

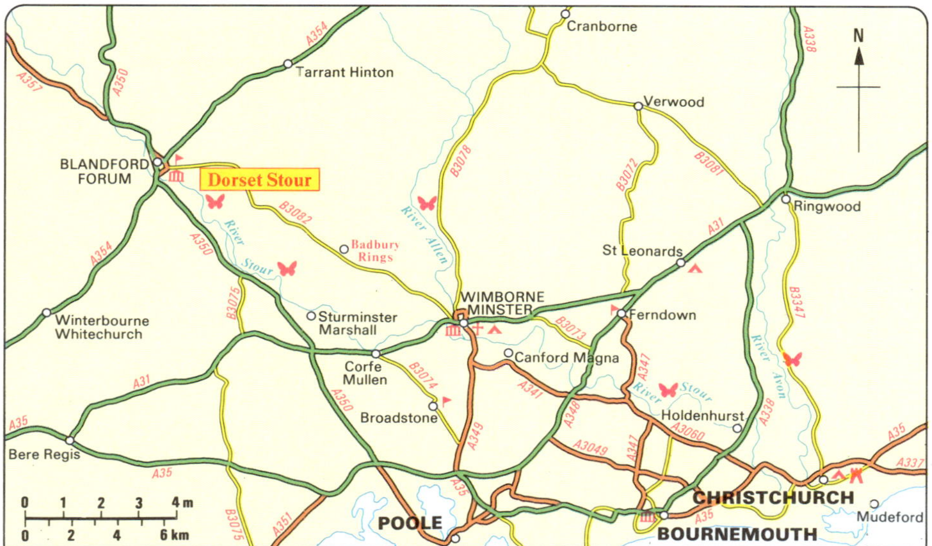

River Allen
Fair mixed fishing, but visitors' chances limited
Daily tickets: The Bull Inn, Wimborne
Water Authority: WWA

River Avon
Top class trout and coarse fishing
Daily tickets: The Bailiff, Avon Buildings, Christchurch (salmon and trout), N Ward, Avon Dairy Farm, The Bridges, Ringwood
Water Authority: as River Allen

nearby *may* have something to do with this phenomenon! Within Blandford Camp is a recently gathered collection of uniforms, papers and mementoes of the renowned Royal Signals regiment.

Angling in and around the town is controlled by local associations and the stranger to these parts may be pleasantly surprised by some very large pike plus the profusion of perch which teem in the waters.

The town marks the end of this featured thirty-mile stretch of the Stour. From here it wends its way on through beautiful rolling Dorset countryside. A word of caution to Hampshire anglers visiting this region – the characters of the Avon and the Stour differ deceptively. So beware of the rapidly varying flows after prolonged rainfall, caused by the heavy Oxford clay which the Stour drains throughout Blackmoor Vale.

Lovers of Thomas Hardy cannot visit Dorset without seeking out his birthplace near Higher Brockhampton. The thatched cottage is tenanted, but it is possible to arrange a viewing.

Camping
Christchurch: Grove Farm Meadow Holiday Caravan Park ►►►►
Tel: (0202) 483597
Level 50-pitch site (no tents)
Open Mar–Oct, no bookings
St Leonards: Camping International ►►►►
Tel: (0202) 872817
Small 60-pitch site off A31
Open Easter–Oct, must book Jul–Aug
Wimborne Minster: Wilksworth Farm Caravan Park ►►►
Tel: (0202) 885467
Flat 85-pitch farmland site
Open Mar–Oct, must book Jul–Aug

Golfing
Blandford: The Ashley Wood
Tel: (0258) 2253
Undulating downland course, 9 holes, 5221yds, par 68, SSS66
Bournemouth: Knighton Heath
Tel: (020 16) 2633
High heathland course, 18 holes, 6227yds, par 70, SSS70
Broadstone:
Tel: (0202) 693363
Heathland course 3m S of Wimborne, 18 holes, 6204yds (5951yds in winter), par 69, SSS70 (69 winter)
Ferndown:
Tel: (0202) 872022
Pretty heather course 5m E of Wimborne, 18 holes, 6423yds, par 70, SSS71

General
Blandford: Royal Signals Museum: recent collection of army signalling methods
Open all year
Mon–Fri 10–5 (Sat by appointment)
Tel: (0258) 2581 ext 248
Bournemouth: British Typewriter Museum: unique collection of over 300 typewriters
Open all year (ex Sun)
Tel: (0202) 21009
Russell-Coates Art Gallery: with special Oriental art section
Open all year (ex Sun) 10.30–5
Christchurch: Tucktonia: fascinating scaled miniatures of British buildings, plus leisure complex
Open Mar–Oct from 10
Tel: (0202) 485100/482710
Wimborne: Badbury Rings: circular Iron Age fortification with splendid beech avenue approach, 4m NW of Wimborne off B3082
Merley Bird Gardens: large outdoor aviary complex
Open all year 10.30–6.30
Tel: (0202) 3790

Kennet and Avon Canal

Hungerford – Bradford on Avon

Water Authorities
Thames Water Authority
Tel: (0734) 593333/593235
Wessex Water Authority
Tel: (0272) 25462/25491

Angling Associations
Bradford on Avon & District Angling Association
Devizes Angling Association
Hungerford Canal Angling Association
Lavington Angling Club
Marlborough & District Angling Association
Pewsey & District Angling Association
St George Angling Club

Close Seasons
TWA: *trout:* October 1 – March 31, *rainbow trout:* December 1 – March 14, *coarse fish:* March 15 – June 15
WWA: *trout:* October 16 – March 31, *coarse fish:* March 15 – June 15

Catch Records
Bream: 10-8-0, *carp:* 14-4-4, *pike:* 21-0-0, *roach:* 2-9-0

It is an indisputable fact that this 170-year-old waterway, linking the River Thames at Reading with the River Avon at Bath, offers the finest canal fishing in Britain.

Regular canal traffic ceased during the Thirties, eventually resulting in many impassable stretches. However, recent concerted preservation work by the Kennet and Avon Canal Trust has opened up several reaches for pleasure boating. Despite anglers' scepticism, there is general agreement that the effect on fishing will be minimal.

The selected thirty eight-mile stretch takes us westward from Hungerford Bridge, where the canal parts company with the River Kennet, a fine fishing place to start. Here the canal is regularly re-stocked with rainbow trout and coarse fish, with chances of tench to 7½lb, bream to 5½lb, roach to 3¼lb and trout to 7lb. Tickets for this area are available from Lambs Hotel, which not only provides comfortable accommodation, but happens to be also the headquarters of the Hungerford Canal Angling Association.

Four locks further on and a little to the north of Froxfield is Littlecote House. It is a large Tudor mansion with an impressive armoury and beautiful gardens and is well worth a visit.

From Froxfield, through Little Bedwyn and on to Great Bedwyn, the canal makes its long ascent. About one and a half miles south west of Great Bedwyn, at Crofton is the now-unique Boulton & Watt beam engine which helps pump water up the forty feet to the next level. Along this stretch, short trips by narrow-boat may be enjoyed during special steam weekends. You can telephone for details. This same stretch of water may yield the odd 10lb bream.

Beyond Crofton Pumphouse, certain parts of the waterway are dry and overgrown, but water reappears at lock 57, approaching Wilton.

To the south of Durley, one mile east of the A346, is the western limit of the Thames Water Authority's jurisdiction, while to the north is the splendid Savernake Forest. The imposing beech avenues, majestic oaks and countless walking trails, *plus* the chance of spotting the odd deer make this region a picnicking paradise.

The canal climbs here to its highest level. The summit of 474 feet above sea level is reached at the first lock beyond Savernake. From Wootton Top, meandering down the Vale of Pewsey and now under the Wessex Water Authority's wing, the canal still offers good chances to the visitor. From Pewsey (where you will no doubt spot the sixty-six foot high White Horse cut into the chalk downs) to Wilcot, a three-mile stretch, daily tickets for some splendid angling are obtainable from the Pewsey Angling Association.

Bream and grayling tend to be predominant in these waters.

For paddle-boat enthusiasts, the *Charlotte Dundas* plies the stretch between Pewsey Wharf and Devizes which is known as the 'long pound'. Details of sailing times are available from the booking manager, who may be reached on *(038 084) 673.*

At nearby Milton Lilbourne, two miles east of Pewsey, the beautiful Milton Manor Gardens, open on Wednesday afternoons throughout the summer, should not be missed.

The fifteen-mile stretch from Lady's Bridge, Wilcot to Semington Bridge offers very good coarse fishing and is regularly re-stocked with above-average bream and tench by the Devizes Angling Association who control the fishing rights of this part of the river.

The top stretch of water past Devizes Hospital may well yield carp up to 20lb, whilst further down, at Seend saw-mills, grayling, rudd and tench are plentiful.

Several inns are sprinkled along this reach, notably the Barge at Honey Street, a plum location where anglers regularly meet and discuss the many pike that get away! Fishermen will also find welcomes at the White Bear, the Castle and the Old Crown. The Devizes club operates an exchange ticket system, so it may be that you still have some mileage from your Avon, Bath, Calne or Chippenham tickets which are all part of the scheme.

While in the Devizes area, students of the past should not miss the journey to Avebury, seven miles north on the A361. The twenty nine-acre megalithic site, incorporating Avebury Ring, is larger and, on the whole, more impressive than the more famous Stonehenge. The National Trust owns the whole area around the site and results of local excavations can be seen in the village museum. Still on an historical tack, the field of a decisive Civil War Battle, Roundway Down, is explorable by foot just two miles north of Devizes. About two miles south west of this battlefield and completing the triangle, is Lakeside, a small thirty-pitch camp site offering April to October pre-booked accommodation.

Leaving Devizes, the canal descends through a series of twenty-nine, now inoperable, locks to the foot of Caen Hill making an impressive towpath spectacle. Close to lock 19 is the Barge Inn where you can try your hand at bar-billiards or just stand outside and watch the occasional canoeists paddlings their way between portages around derelict locks, obviously enjoying the hazards.

From this point the canal is now flanked by the fast-flowing River Avon and controlled by the Bradford on Avon and District Angling Association. Chances of a catch become rather sparse towards Bradford, but good bream (4½lb – 6lb) can be had around Waddon.

Semington Brook, an offshoot of the Avon, is a popular patch for short-stay anglers offering varied coarse and trout fishing. Daily tickets are issued by the Lavington Angling Association. At the brook's northern end is the sleepy village of Holt where a 300-year-old house with skilfully-hedged gardens, The Courts, may be viewed on weekday afternoons during the summer.

On reaching Bradford on Avon you cannot fail to be fascinated by its maze of narrow,

Camping
Potterne: Potterne Wick Touring Caravan Park ►►►
Tel: (0380) 3277
Grassy 30-pitch site 2m S of Devizes
Open Apr–Oct, must book Jul–Aug
Rowde: Lakeside ►►►
Tel: (0380) 2767
Flat, 30-pitch campsite 2m NW of Devizes
Open Apr–Oct, must book

Golfing
Calne: North Wilts
Tel: (038 086) 627
Lofty downland course 1m SE of Calne, 18 holes, 6451yds, par 72, SSS71
RAF Upavon
Tel: (098 063) 351 ext 232
Windy downland course, 9 holes, 5116yds, par 69, SSS67
Warminster: West Wiltshire
Tel: (0985) 2110
Windswept hilltop course, 18 holes, 5732yds, par 70, SSS68

Riding
Calne: Hampsley Hollow Riding Centre
Tel: (038 085) 333

Walking Trails
The Woodland Park Trails: various 1–2m signposted walks within 80-acre forest region. Start from Brokerswood, Rudge 3m W of Westbury off A36

General
Avebury: Avebury Manor: fine Tudor mansion
Open May & Sep (Sat & Sun) and Jun–Aug daily 2.30–5.30
Avebury Museum: finds from the huge nearby megalithic circle & site
Open all year
Gt Bedwyn: Crofton Beam Engines: two very rare steam-operated pumping engines, narrow-boat canal trips on steam weekends
Tel: (0672) 810474 for details
Holt: The Courts: late 17th-century house with topiary & tree-gardens
Open Apr–Oct 2–6.30 (ex Sat & Sun)
Hungerford: Littlecote House: Tudor manor with unique Cromwellian armour collection, 2m NW of town
Open Apr–Sep (Sat & Sun) 2–6, plus party booking
Tel: (048 86) 2509
Pewsey: Milton Manor Gardens: attractive landscaped gardens
Open May–Oct (Wed only) 2–6
Tel: (067 26) 3344
Savernake Forest: very beautiful woodland region with many riding & walking paths, situated SE of Marlborough

A satisfying specimen of Summer Chub

twisting streets. Many fine Georgian buildings grace the town that was once a thriving wool centre, an indication that just a few miles north west as the crow flies, lies the Mecca of Georgian architecture, Bath. Our journey's end is just west of Bradford at the 168-foot-long 14th-century Barton Farm tithe barn on the Wiltshire-Avon border.

The regular river angler should bear in mind that for the whole of its Hungerford to Bradford stretch, the Kennet and Avon is rarely more than three feet deep. Consequently, the best results will be achieved well down on the bank. Maggots or worms are the best bait.

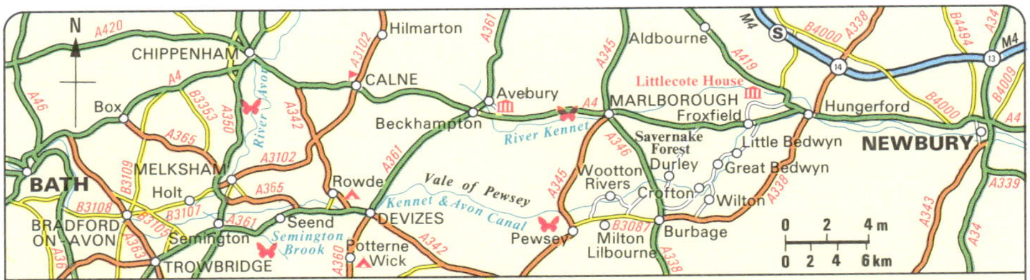

River Avon
Recently re-stocked with barbel towards Bath, but visitors' chances limited
Daily tickets: Bath Angling Association, 30 Charles Street, Bath
Water Authority: WWA

River Kennet
Highly-rated for trout and coarse fishing, but very limited access
Water Authority: TWA

Semington Brook
Good mixed fishing with fair chances for the visitor, from 3m S of Devizes to Holt
Daily tickets: Lavington Angling Club

Angler's Directory for the West of England

Clubs and Associations

Barnstaple & District Angling Association (A J Tyacke), 5 The Bank, Landkey, Barnstaple, Devon

Bideford & District Angling Club (V B Eveleigh), 21 Capern Road, Bideford, Devon
Tel: (023 72) 2470

Blandford & District Angling Association (J Bell), 15 Albert Street, Blandford, Dorset

Bradford-on-Avon & District Angling Association (B Webster), 6 Lyneham Way, Trowbridge, Wiltshire
Tel: (022 14) 62263

Christchurch Angling Club (E G Chislett), Nimrod Sports Ltd, 9 Castle Parade, Iford, Bournemouth
Tel: (020 15) 78224

Devizes Angling Association (K Nisbeck), Park View Cottage, Bath Road, Devizes, Wiltshire

Dulverton Angling Association (F J Stanton), 15 Pixton Way, Dulverton, Somerset

Durweston Angling Society (J H Thatchell), Hethody, Durweston, Blandford, Dorset
Tel: (0258) 54803

Ilfracombe & District Angling Association (Labbetts), 61–62 High Street, Ilfracombe, Devon
Tel: (0271) 62974

Lavington Angling Club (M Gilbert), Gable Cottage, 24 High Street, Erlestoke, Devizes, Wiltshire
Tel: (038 083) 425

Liskeard & District Angling Club (B G Wilson), The Bruff, Callington, Cornwall
Tel: (0579) 62449

Looe Sea Angling Association (V Sharpe), Looe, Cornwall
Tel: (050 36) 2130

Lostwithiel Fishing Association (S G Brewer), Hillhouse, Lostwithiel, Cornwall

Marlborough & District Angling Association (M Ellis), 8 South View, Marlborough, Wiltshire
Tel: (0672) 2922

Mevagissey Sea Angling Club (HQ), The Ship Inn, Pentewan, Mevagissey, Cornwall

Pewsey & District Angling Association (P Bewley), 11 Chisenbury Court, East Chisenbury, Pewsey, Wiltshire

Southampton Piscatorial Society (B Blakey), 14 Furzedale Park, Hythe, Southampton, Hampshire
Tel: (0703) 844042

Tiverton Fly Fishing Club (County Sports), 9 William Street, Tiverton, Devon
Tel: (084 42) 4770

Wimborne & District Angling Club (S A Card), 81 Leigh Lane, Wimborne, Dorset
Tel: (0202) 884986

Tackle Shops

Barnstaple
The Rod Room, 93 Boutport Street
Tel: (0271) 5360

Bideford
B & K Angling, The Quay
Tel: (023 72) 4613
D Foley, 25 Brookfield Street
Tel: (023 72) 3328

Blandford
A Conyers, West Street
Tel: (0258) 52307

Bournemouth
Nimrod Sports Ltd, 5 Castle Parade, Iford
Tel: (020 15) 78224

Christchurch
Davis Fishing Tackle, 75 Bargates
Tel: (0202) 485169
Taylor's Tackle, 258 Barrack Road
Tel: (0202) 484518

Devizes
M Etheridge, 11 Sidmouth Street
F Giles, Lakeside, Rowde
Tel: (0380) 2767
S Nott & Sons, 24 The Brittox
Tel: (0380) 2434

Dulverton
Lance Nicholson Fishing, High Street
Tel: (0398) 23405
H V Tout, High Street

Fowey
James Reid, 10 Esplanade
Tel: (072 683) 2207

Ilfracombe
Sports Centre, 135 High Street
Tel: (0271) 64546

Looe
Jack Bray, The Quay
Tel: (050 36) 2504
The Tackle Shop (Shark Fishing), East Looe
Tel: (050 36) 2189

Lynton
Angler's Corner, Castle Hill

Marlborough
H Duck, High Street

Mevagissey
Dunn Bros, West Wharf
The Tackle Box, 13 Fore Street
Tel: (072 684) 3513

Pewsey
T Kemp, Canal House, Marlborough Road
Odd Jobs Ltd, 10–16 High Street
Tel: (067 26) 2403

St Austell
The Angling Centre, 6 Victoria Place
Tel: (0726) 63377

South Molton
Thompson's, 6 Broad Street

Tiverton
County Sports, 9 William Street
Tel: (084 42) 4770
Penfold Sports & Leisure, 4 Market Precinct Wychware, Newport Street

Trowbridge
S H Davies Tackle Shop, 32 Rounstone Street
Tel: (022 14) 5472
C W Rose & Son, 6 Fore Street

Wimborne
John March Fishing Tackle, 19 West Borough
Tel: (0202) 888504
Minster Sports, 8 West Street
Tel: (0202) 882240
W H Newman, The Boat House, Canford Bridge
Tel: (0202) 883443

Water Authorities

South West Water Authority, 3–5 Barnfield Road, Exeter, Devon
Tel: (0392) 31666

Thames Water Authority, 2nd Floor, Reading Bridge House, Reading, Berkshire
Tel: (0734) 593333

Wessex Water Authority, Techno House, Redcliffe Way, Bristol, Avon
Tel: (0272) 25462/25491

Fisheries

Exe Valley Fisheries, Dulverton, Somerset
Tel: (0398) 23328

Royalty Fishery (West Hants Water Company), Knapp Mill, Christchurch, Dorset
Tel: (0202) 483361

Throop Fishery, South Lodge, Holdenhurst, Bournemouth, Dorset
Tel: (0202) 35532

Wimbleball, Upton, Dulverton, Somerset
Tel: (039 87) 209

Hotels and Inns

Bideford
New Inn
Tel: (023 72) 2810
Royal Hotel
Tel: (023 72) 2005

Blandford
Star Inn
Tel: (0258) 52108

Christchurch
King's Arms Hotel
Tel: (0202) 484117

Clovelly
New Inn
Tel: (023 73) 222
Red Lion
Tel: (023 73) 308

Devizes
Barge Inn, Honey Street

Dulverton
Caernarvon Arms Hotel
Tel: (0398) 23302
Lamb Hotel
Tel: (0398) 23369

Exebridge
Anchor Inn
Tel: (0398) 23433

Fowey
Ship Hotel
Tel: (072 683) 2230

Lostwithiel
Royal Talbot
Tel: (0208) 872498

Polperro
Claremount Hotel
Tel: (0503) 72536

Simonsbath
Exmoor Forest Hotel
Tel: (064 383) 341

Tiverton
Hartnoll Country House Hotel
Tel: (088 42) 2777

Wimborne
Three Lions Hotel

South East & East Midlands 2

Isle of Wight Coast and Southampton Water

Angling Associations
Christchurch Angling Club
Isle of Wight Angling Society
Shanklin Angling Society
Vectis Boating and Fishing Club
Ventnor Angling Club

Tackle Dealers
Bates & Son, 5 Spring Hill, Ventnor
Davis Fishing Tackle, 75 Bargate, Christchurch
Patstone & Cox Ltd, 25 High Street, Southampton
Sea-Tac, 8 Wilkes Road, Sandown
Smiths Sports Shop, 25 Queen Street, Lymington
The Tackle Box, 73 High Street, Ryde

HM Coastguard
Bembridge: *Tel: (098 387) 2886*
Fawley: *Tel: (0703) 893574*
Freshwater: *Tel: (098 383) 2265*
Hayling Island: *Tel: (070 16) 4095*
Selsey: *Tel: (024 361) 2274*
Southampton: *Tel: (0703) 8091*

Inland Fishing Water Authority
Wessex Water Authority
Tel: Bristol (0272) 25491

The mainland coast from Selsey Bill to Hurst Beach, separated from the Isle of Wight by the Solent and Spithead, offers some of the most varied saltwater fishing in the South of England. The whole area lent strength to the sea angling boom of the Sixties – newcomers to the sport found they could come here and try many different fishing styles in nearly ideal surroundings. They caught fish, and the fame of the Solent was assured.

While some claim this popularity left the area barren, the hundreds of anglers who still enjoy its miles of harbour and estuary shore, the superb casting beaches and the wisdom of the many experienced charter-boat skippers testify to its continuing worth. The coast is not all harbours, beaches and boats. There are also small, shallow bays fringed with salt grass, long banks and sea defences fronting deep water when the tide is up. The great triple estuary of Southampton Water, where the Rivers Test, Itchen and Hamble empty over banks and through channels, is also home to everything that swims from all sizes of flatfish to migrating trout and salmon.

All the sheltered and enclosed inshore waters of the Solent are good for mullet, bass, small pollack, flounders and seasonal catches such as black bream and mackerel. The occasional big conger is hauled from deep holes near wrecks and stonework and some codling are taken from the entrance channels in winter. A good tip for bay fishing is to look for mullet and flounders inside the prolific salt grass (fishing from the shore) and to use a boat for bass outside the salt grass. Fishing in sheltered water during the summer is made difficult by crabs which rapidly strip ledgered baits – use a float to lift the bait just above the bottom. Light tackle is essential if your quarry is the wily soft-mouthed mullet.

The favourite bait over the whole area is the Southampton King Ragworm, dug out from local estuarine mud. Other baits, all good at times, are harbour rag, lugworm, slipper-limpet, soft crab and bread paste. Use rag, with or without an attractive spoon, for flounders and bass, and bread paste in a ground-baited area for mullet. Sand-eel, squid and strips of herring or mackerel will sometimes take big bass from fast-flowing channels or entice conger from the stonework of Portsmouth Harbour and Southampton Docks. Pier and harbour fishing can be enjoyed at Chichester, Langstone, Portsmouth, Lymington (the outer banks) and the many other smaller quays to be found in the area.

Most of the shoreline outside harbours is good for beach-casting. Baits such as rag and lug worms will catch bass, stingrays, pollack, flatfish, mackerel and bream in season. Codling appear in winter and there is the occasional surprise catch of a decent-sized cod (Hurst Castle is the spot for this). A long cast from Hurst Beach will reach one of the south coast's best bass grounds; sand-eel is the deadly bait here, but by all means try fish strips and squid in winter. Among the best beach-casting places are Selsey Bill, South Hayling (try Eastoke Point) and the whole coast from Southampton Water to Lymington and Hurst Beach.

Favourite marks for charter boats include the Shingles bank (a bass ground extending from Hurst Castle into the Solent's west arm); the one-, two-, and three-mile gullies scoring the seabed off West Wight (these are incoming cod routes); and the famous shark grounds off St Catherine's Point. As a rule of thumb, the water south of the Isle of Wight yields really big fish – in the Solent fish are smaller and of fewer species. Summer feathering used to yield large mackerel catches but commercial fishing has depleted stocks seriously in recent years throughout the area.

Details of charter boats are available from all local tackle shops, but most experts will point to the quays at Lymington, Keyhaven and Yarmouth as having consistent records. Many quays operate eight hour trips day or night, all year round, weather permitting. But there is fun for all the family in the three-hour mackerel trips operated from June to September.

This whole region is a vast holiday playground,

Boating a tope

so few family members should be at a loose end while the anglers are away. If your holiday base is on the Isle of Wight, local transport for those without cars is no problem. The island is only twenty-two miles long and thirteen miles wide and it is well-covered by the Southern Vectis bus company and the ex-London tube trains of the Ryde-Shanklin-Sandown railway.

Sun-seekers can aim for the wide beaches of Shanklin, Sandown, Ventnor and Freshwater which offer good bathing and the back-up of bustling resort facilities. Throughout August, the towns are host to a series of carnivals but, for onlookers, some of the most spectacular sights are the yachts congregating for the island's many sailing events. Cowes has a packed programme of weekend regattas from April–September climaxing in the famous Cowes Week during July.

While the coast lures the attentions of many visitors, the heart of the island can be as lonely as any stretch of beautiful countryside. This is marvellous walking country with over a thousand footpaths and bridleways to discover. Rolling downland, intimate farm clusters and extensive woods have their own wild-life species, peculiar to the island, to reveal. The Granville Fritillary is a rare and ornate butterfly. Here the red squirrel is almost untroubled by the grey species so predominant on the mainland. Botanists will hunt the wild calamint, a fragrant cousin of mint and thyme. Serious walkers will attempt the island's sixty-five-mile coastal path with its dramatic views of the rugged south coast and the large populations of guillemots, razorbills and kittiwakes.

This is just one aspect of the island's conservationist face. At Yafford Water Mill Farm Park (near Shorwell, south west of Newport) is a 'rare breeds survival centre', with a collection of waterfowl living on a large mill pond set in the middle of an attractive park. There is also a collection of farm implements, wagons and tractors. More waterfowl are to be found at the Flamingo Park Sanctuary, Seaview, in rolling countryside overlooking the Solent – many of the birds will feed from visitors' hands if they exercise particular care.

If children fail to find the Ryde tube trains fascinating enough there is the real thing at Haven Street a few miles inland. Here a former LSWR tank engine of 1891 vintage steams through two miles of island countryside with static displays of other engines and rolling stock. But as nobody can ever be far from the sea it is the boats that will draw families to the sea ports. As a reminder of the island's principal industry in time gone by, Ventnor houses a unique tribute to private enterprise. It is the Museum of Smuggling – a display of 700 years of cunning methods and devices to beat Customs and Excise.

Just as these illicit sea traders knew, the island is a fortress beset by strong and unpredictable tides and currents. The warning to all sea anglers, and particularly those in boats, is that great care must be taken. An untutored skipper attempting to fish the Shingles or the navigable channels off West Wight courts trouble. Small-boaters should take plenty of local advice or you, too, could inadvertently find yourself among the many wrecks that litter these coasts and harbours.

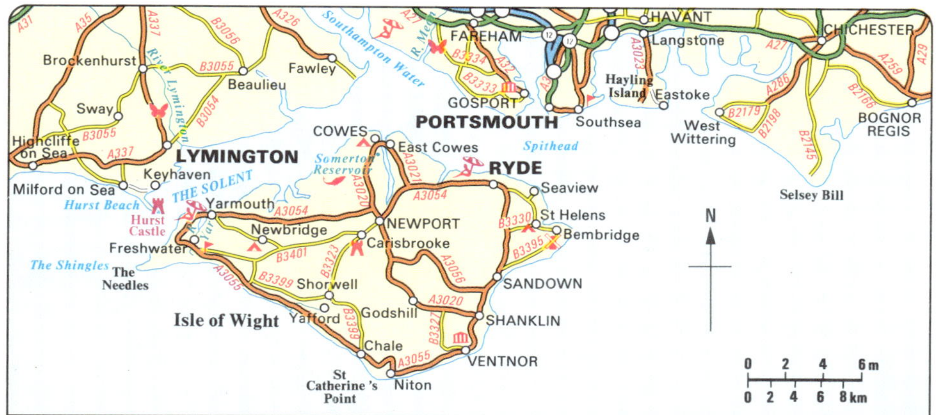

River Lymington
Fair trout fishing
Daily tickets (in advance): Smith's Sports and Tackle Shop, Lymington
Forestry Commission (riparian owner), The Queens House, Lyndhurst
No licence required

River Meon
Good stream for brown trout
Daily tickets (in advance): Hansford's, Fareham
Water Authority: SWA

Somerton Reservoirs
Another Isle of Wight coarse fishery
Daily tickets: as River Yar
Water Authority: as River Meon

River Yar
Upper reaches yield trout, whilst most coarse fish are present lower down
Daily tickets: Isle of Wight Freshwater Angling Association
Water Authority: as River Meon

Camping
Cowes: Thorness Bay Holiday Village ▶▶▶
Tel: (0983) 523109
Level, grassy 200-pitch caravan site
Open Easter–Oct, no bookings
Newbridge: Orchards Holiday Caravan Park ▶▶▶▶
Tel: (098 378) 331
Gently sloping 175-pitch site
Open May–Sep, must book Jul–Aug
St Helens: Nodes Point Holiday Village ▶▶▶
Tel: (098 387) 2401
Slightly sloping 250-pitch tent site
Open mid-May–Sep, must book Jul–Aug

Golfing
Freshwater Bay
Tel: (098 383) 2400
Pleasant links course, off A3055, 18 holes, 5504yds, par 67, SSS67
Southsea
Tel: (0705) 60945
Meadowland course with easy walking, 18 holes, 6018yds, par 72, SSS69

Walking Trails
Brook Nature Trail: 1¾m (1hr) circular woodland walk abounding with flowers. Start from Brook, IoW, midway between A3055 & B3399
Fort Victoria Country Park Nature Trail: 1¼m (1½hr) signposted coastal walk leading back to exhibition room. Start from Fort Victoria Cafe, Westhill Lane, ½m W of Yarmouth off A3054

General
Bembridge:
Bembridge Windmill: all machinery intact, only windmill on IoW
Open Apr–Sep daily 10–5 (Sun 11–6)
Carisbrooke:
Carisbrooke Castle: partly 12th-century fortress now housing IoW museum
Open all year (museum closed Oct–Easter)
Cowes: Curds & Whey: daily talks on cheese-making at Dottens Farm
Open Easter–Sep (11.30 & 2.30)
Tel: (0983) 292466
East Cowes: Barton Manor Gardens & Vineyard: grounds & lake with 5-acre vineyard, wine-tasting.
Open Easter–May (Sun only), then Jun–Sep daily
Tel: (0983) 292835
Gosport: Submarine Museum: vast display of submarines, models, medals, etc
Open all year 9–4 (ex Sun) by prior arrangement only
Tel: (0705) 22351 ext 41868
Portsmouth: Ford Widley: Napoleonic invasion fortress with maze of underground passages
Open Apr–Sep daily 2–6
HMS Victory: Nelson's famous flagship restored to Trafalgar conditions
Open Mar–Oct 10.30–5.30 (Sun 1–5), winter 10.30–4.30 (Sun 1–4.30)
Tel: (0705) 22351 ext 23111

Kent Coast

Deal – Margate

Angling Associations
Broadstairs & St Peter's Sea Angling Society
Deal Angling Club
Deal & Walmer Angling Association
Margate Fishing Club
Old Centrals Angling Club
Royal Ramsgate Invicta Angling Club
Sandwich & District Angling Society

Tackle Dealers
The Angler, 19 King Street, Deal
Fisherman's Workshop, 66 Oxford Street, Ramsgate
Fo'csle Tackle Stores, 33 Beach Street, Deal
Geoff's, 36 Fort Hill, Margate
Kingfisheries, 34 King Street, Margate
Ramsgate Bait & Tackle, 7 Westcliff Arcade, Ramsgate

HM Coastguard
Dover/Deal: *Tel: (0304) 210008*
Ramsgate/Margate: *Tel: (0843) 20807*

Inland Fishing Water Authority
Southern Water Authority
Tel: Worthing (0903) 205252

For the frustrated angler in Central London, the coastline of east Kent provides the ideal answer. It is accessible – Deal is just two to three hours' drive away, via the M2 – and, as a bonus, boasts some of the best sea angling in the country. In fact, anglers come from much farther afield than the Home Counties to try these waters. The North Sea, ebbing and flowing through the Straits of Dover, makes for some ferocious tides in these parts, but this is compensated by the water's relative shallowness. Rarely is it deeper than fourteen fathoms making for relatively safe fishing.

In Deal itself, there is good fishing all the year round, with just about every species of sea fish caught at some time in these waters. Spring is the time for dogfish and skate, then during the summer, bass, black bream, mackerel and very good tope are in attendance. It is from September to December, though, that Deal becomes *the* place for anglers to be. The port is renowned for its quality whiting, flounder, sole and cod, the latter occasionally topping a record 20lb or so.

In 1957 a new 1 000-foot pier was built at Deal and has since been the focal point for keen anglers. To the south, off adjoining Walmer, sorties to fish wrecks around the hazardous Goodwin Sands have opened up good conger possibilities, whilst northward, good plaice can be had. Traditional methods here tend to produce the best results, but it is as well to mention that a very long trace is advisable for cod and skate. Locally recommended bait is good old lugworm, plus soft crab and squid if available.

Further up the coast is Pegwell Bay, a good spot for dab, thornback and whiting. During the summer, large shoals of mullet enter the local harbour and are easily caught on freshwater tackle. This bay has a high reputation for its shrimps, but amateur netters should beware of the treacherous sands. Bait may be dug in this area or gathered from the rocks.

At the southern end of the bay is the Stour

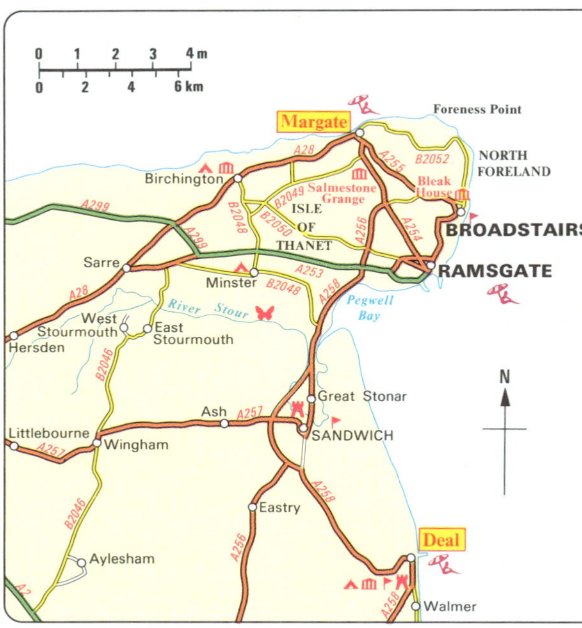

Deal
Shore and boat fishing for bass, cod, flounder, mullet, sole, whiting
Tackle shop: The Angler, 19 King Street, Deal
Tel: (030 45) 4573

Margate
Excellent shore fishing with cod, dab, mullet, plaice, tope. By boat: conger, bream, ray, turbot
Tackle shop: Geoff's Fishing Tackle, 36 Fort Hill, Margate
Tel: (0843) 26386

Ramsgate
Good shore fishing, especially towards Stour estuary – including flounder, mackerel, whiting
Tackle shop: Fisherman's Corner, 6 Kent Place, Ramsgate
Tel: (0843) 582174

River Stour
Various coarse fish plus sea trout, but chances limited
Free fishing from Sandwich to estuary
Water Authority: SWA
Tel: (0903) 205252

Fishing boats at Broadstairs

Camping
Birchington: Quex Caravan & Camping Park ►
Tel: (0843) 41273
Small 150-pitch site
Open Mar–Oct, no bookings
Deal: Sutton Vale Caravan Park ►►►
Tel: (01 837) 1093 (Mon–Fri)
Small 28-pitch caravan-only site
Open Apr–Sep, must book Jul–Aug
Minster: Wayside Caravan Park ►►
Tel: (0843) 821272
Compact 10-pitch site (no tents)
Open Mar–Oct, no bookings

Golfing
Broadstairs: North Foreland:
Tel: (0843) 62140
Scenic seaside course, 18 holes, 6378yds, par 71, SSS70
Deal: Royal Cinque Ports:
Tel: (030 45) 4007
Windy seaside course, 18 holes, 6384yds, par 70, SSS72
Ramsgate: St Augustine's:
Tel: (0843) 821346
Fairly flat seaside course, 18 holes, 5018yds, par 69, SSS65
Sandwich: Prince's:
Tel: (030 46) 2000
Very good links course, 18 holes, 6950yds, par 73, SSS73

General
Birchington: Powell Cotton Museum: natural history with huge stuffed animals
Open Easter–Sep (Wed, Thur & Sun)
Tel: (0843) 42168
Deal: Deal Castle: 16th-century stronghold with pottery & Iron Age weapon exhibits
Open all year
Maritime & Local History Museum: recently opened collection of seafaring items
Open May–Sep daily 2–5
Tel: (030 45) 4524
Margate: Salmestone Grange: restored mediaeval house
Open May–Sep (Sat only 2–5) or by appointment
Tel: (0843) 21136
Sandwich: Guildhall: restored 16th-century building with local relics & documents
Open all year
Tel: (030 46) 2200/3060

estuary. The ancient port of Sandwich is now no less than two miles up-river, but sea fishing is still quite profitable to the north of the ever-growing Sandwich Flats. Optimum angling periods here are two hours either side of high tide, with bass, dab and big congers the most likely catches. On the Stour itself, sea trout and mullet are of good size and there is free fishing along the stretch from Sandwich to the main estuary. There is ticket angling through clubs for most coarse fish further on upstream (fly fishing is not recommended though, as the water is too coloured).

Back to the open sea and upon the 'Isle' of Thanet, the first major town reached is Ramsgate. The harbour area is the busiest part of town, not now as a fishing port, but as an import-export centre for cars and mixed cargoes. However, some ship-repairing is still carried out here. The large beaches offer good sport during the summer, but tend to be overcrowded, so you will find night angling more enjoyable – and more profitable. Inshore boatmen are at your service for bass, cod, flounder and sole. But if you care to venture farther out to sea, Elbow Buoy is an exceptionally good location for cod in the winter and the North Goodwins, seven miles due east of Ramsgate, is a prime summer spot for thornback.

When the tide is out, the two miles between Ramsgate and Broadstairs can be pleasurably walked along the sands. The many rock-pools encountered on this stretch have given many a youngster his first taste of angling. Bass and pouting are the species most likely to take the bait either from this shore at the chalk ledges or from Broadstairs' very old pier, whilst from a boat you can add cod, plaice, tope and whiting.

About a mile off Foreness Point, the north-eastern tip of Thanet, is Longnose Buoy, where dinghy anglers can anticipate more top-rate cod plus conger. The summer fishing here, for bass off the inshore chalk ledges (using artificial lures), can be very profitable.

Another mile along the coast brings you within Margate's town boundary. Several species offer themselves within a very short distance at this pleasant seaside resort. Off the quarter-of-a-mile wooden jetty, mullet are prevalent, whilst big flatfish catches are commonplace on the sand at Newfoundland Rocks. By the central stretch of shore, bass (on paternoster line) and some dab can be expected. At Minnis Bay, Birchington, to the west of Margate, skate is the most likely catch. Boats may be hired from the harbour and if it is tope that you are after, then June is the month.

Whilst in Margate, the more energetic may like to visit Dreamland, a vast complex including a scenic railway, rides, shows and even a safari park. In a quieter vein, Salmestone Grange, to the south, provides a very good example of a restored monastery.

Back past the North Foreland Lighthouse, Broadstairs possesses one of the best seaside golf links in the South. The long North Foreland course combines easy walking with testing holes. On the town's north cliff is *the* Bleak House, immortalised by Charles Dickens. Buffs of this author can delve deeper at the local Dickens House Museum which displays a wealth of his memorabilia.

Ramsgate boasts several well-kept gardens and lawns, notably Madeira Walk and Winterstoke Gardens, the latter of which overlooks the harbour. Here the Royal Temple Yacht Club has its headquarters, and holds a regatta each August.

Places of interest in Sandwich include Richborough Castle and the Guildhall, a surprisingly interesting public records building. But the town's architectural pearl is the Barbican, an old toll-house with its lower half alternately-bricked, chessboard fashion.

Thanks to Henry VIII's coastal fortress-building zeal, Deal owns a combined national monument and museum. The walls of the town's castle, twenty feet thick at the base of the bastions, made it surely the toughest 16th-century nut to crack.

So having cast a glance at possible places to visit, it only remains for you to cast a line out from this very pleasant angling stretch of the Kent coast and take a good catch.

Essex Stour

Harwich – Sudbury

Water Authority
Anglian Water Authority – Essex division licence required
Tel: (0480) 56181 or Divisional office Chelmsford *(0245) 64721*

Angling Associations
London Anglers' Association
Sudbury and District Angling Society
Colchester Angling Preservation Society
Colnes Angling Society
Hadleigh and District Angling Society

Tackle shops
Home & Sports, Colchester
Sudbury Sports, Sudbury
The Swim, Sudbury

Close Season
Coarse fish: March 15 – June 15

Forming the border between the counties of Essex and Suffolk, the River Stour and its environs once gave endless inspiration to the painter John Constable. The artistic connections continue with Gainsborough who was born at Sudbury, a fine old market town on the river, and Sir Alfred Munnings, best known for his portraits of equine champions, who lived and worked at Castle House, Dedham, some miles to the east.

Meandering for some forty miles from the marshy lands of the estuary near Harwich past Flatford Mill and many more of Constable's favourite subjects, the Stour is a small river but eminently fishable for most coarse species. Roach, dace, bream, chub and pike are plentiful and the brackish estuarial waters support large populations of mullet and flounders. However, proximity to London and keen local anglers have reduced the facilities available to visiting fishermen and the weekending or holiday angler is well-advised to check on the availability of tickets in advance – the local tackle shops are, of course, the best source of this knowledge.

Perhaps the biggest challenge the river has to offer is the search for a specimen chub. Fish of three or four pounds are taken regularly from some of the Stour's noted chub areas. But these are fish which tend to keep close in to overhanging bushes and tree roots. Really accurate casting is the only way to draw them out. Keep a very low profile on the bank and be prepared to move around as you will only be able to take one fish or, at best, two from any one swim before moving on. Spend time fishing deep spots close to undercut banks and in parts where the flow is forced between weed beds.

Perhaps the best way to enjoy this kind of fishing is to join the London Anglers' Association which has extensive rights to Stour waters and has an open membership. The London Anglers' Association has only one day-ticket stretch, at Bures, but there are several other beats of the river available, the ticket money being an important revenue source to local clubs. Around Flatford Mill itself are two stretches, the lower river at Brantham and Cattawade offers two more stretches (from the barrage to the sea is free) and there are available sections at Dedham, Great Henny and Sudbury. Bank patrolling bailiffs sell tickets in the Sudbury to Long Melford area.

This last stretch, accessible from the A134, is noted for some excellent bream to be taken

Camping
East Bergholt: Grange Caravan Park ►►►
Tel: (020 629) 567
Grassy 148-pitch site (48 tents)
Open Apr–Sep, no bookings

Golfing
Sudbury: Newton Green
Tel: (0787) 75601
Flat heathland course, 9 holes, 5442yds, par 69, SSS66
Stoke-by-Nayland:
Tel: (0206) 262836
Undulating vale course 9m N of Colchester, 18 holes, 6430yds, par 72, SSS71

Riding
Dedham: Valley Riding School & Stud, Mill Lane
Sudbury: The Paddocks Riding School, Abbey Villa, Abbey Road
Tel: (0787) 76320 day (72004 night)

General
Colchester: Colchester Zoo: Stanway Hall: modern zoo with aquarium & birdland plus model railway
Open all year daily 9.30–7.30
Tel: (0206) 330253
The Minories: Georgian House now a gallery & visual arts centre
Open all year (ex Mon)
Tel: (0206) 77067
Dedham: Castle House: former home & studio of the painter Sir Alfred Munnings
Open May–mid-Oct (Wed & Sun) or by arrangement
Tel: (0206) 322127
East Bergholt: Flatford Lock: restored lock used by non-powered craft
Open at all times – for party demonstrations contact: F Batten, Wissington Grove, Nayland
Harwich: The Redoubt: large circular fort built in the Napoleonic era
Open Easter–Oct 10–12 & 2–5 (Sun only)
Mistley: Mistley Towers: twin porticoed towers, remains of 18th-century church 1m E of Manningtree
Accessible all year
Sudbury: Gainsborough's House: the painter's birthplace, now an art gallery & museum
Open all year (ex Mon) – Sun afternoons only
Tel: (0787) 72958

by float fishing or ledgering techniques. While dace and roach shoal in the shallower parts of the river, it is the many swims of up to seven feet deep that harbour the bream. Float-fish in these pools with maggot bait, worms or bread. If you are using ledger tackle with maggot or worms, eels can be a considerable nuisance throughout the Stour.

The river's dace and roach should not be ignored. Both species run to a very good size and make more exciting fishing if time is limited and you lack the range to explore for the swims of the bigger fish. Use the lightest possible tackle for the best results.

Holiday anglers moving inland from the coastal resorts such as Clacton and Frinton will find the river's lower reaches easily accessible from the B1070, the A137 and the B1352. Fishing bread paste for mullet is the favourite technique among local rods and this shy fish will give the expert, using fine tackle, plenty to think about. For the flounders – which make a tasty holiday meal – a small spoon baited with a piece of ragworm fluttering behind should bring results. Summer estuary anglers should spot some good bass working their way round the banks. A ragworm should tempt them.

To tempt the rest of the family, the area of the Stour extends from the coastal resort towns of Clacton, Frinton and Walton on the Naze and between the regional centres of Colchester and Ipswich. Frinton and Walton, standing together on the coast south of the continental ferry port of Harwich, are typical Victorian resorts. Frinton is by far the more sedate of the two (even today there are no pubs in the town limits) but both have fine sandy beaches with safe bathing. Walton Backwaters and Horsey Island are a wilderness of creeks and tidal salt fens, the habitat for numerous unusual species of birds and the inspiration for Arthur Ransome's children's adventure story *Secret Water*.

Clacton has the full facilities of a modern resort including a zoo, dolphinarium, cinemas, swimming and pleasure plane trips. North of the Stour and Orwell estuaries is the equally attractive resort of Felixstowe, now fast becoming a major docks and export centre to rival Harwich. The German Empress Augusta first made it fashionable (in 1891) although it is more appreciated now for its sandy beach with very little tidal movement.

If you dislike staying in large resorts, there are many campsites and delightful self-catering holiday cottages in the countryside behind the coastline. A beachside site is at St Osyth near Clacton, in the heart of Constable's country there is a site at East Bergholt and north of Felixstowe is the Moon & Sixpence, a full facilities site named after the Somerset Maugham novel.

The Stour is not just the home of the painter. This was an area where both milling and woollen cloth weaving flourished. While the mills, of which the most famous is, of course, Flatford, are still to be found, much of the evidence of the cloth trade has vanished. What remains are the many fine 'woollen' churches endowed with opulent architecture and rich in carvings paid for by the rich weavers. Dedham church, with a spire that broached the skyline of many Constable masterpieces, is thought to be one of the finest of these 15th–16th-century monuments to prosperity. Dedham's mill featured in the Domesday Book. Castle House (open at most holiday times) was Munnings' home and contains many examples of his work. Other churches rivalling Dedham in splendour are at Stoke-by-Nayland (another Constable subject), Stratford St Mary and Brantham. East Bergholt church has links with Cardinal Wolsey – because its tower was never finished the bells were built into an unusual carrillon cage in the graveyard at ground level.

Flatford Mill and Willie Lott's cottage are now a Field Studies Council centre closed to the public. You can still stroll along the adjacent bridleway and visit Flatford Lock, a restored section of the partially-canalised Stour in use by non-powered craft. Transport history of another kind is on view at Castle Hedingham near Sudbury where six locomotives of the Colne Valley Railway and a number of old buildings have been restored by enthusiasts who steam up the engines for short rides at weekends and Bank Holidays. You could return to a coastal base via Colchester. Stanway Hall, three miles west of the town on the A12 is a zoo and amusement park with a large collection of big cats, model railway systems and well-planned picnic areas. What better welcome back to your holiday campsite or cottage than a dinner of fresh-caught flounders?

A peaceful afternoon's fishing

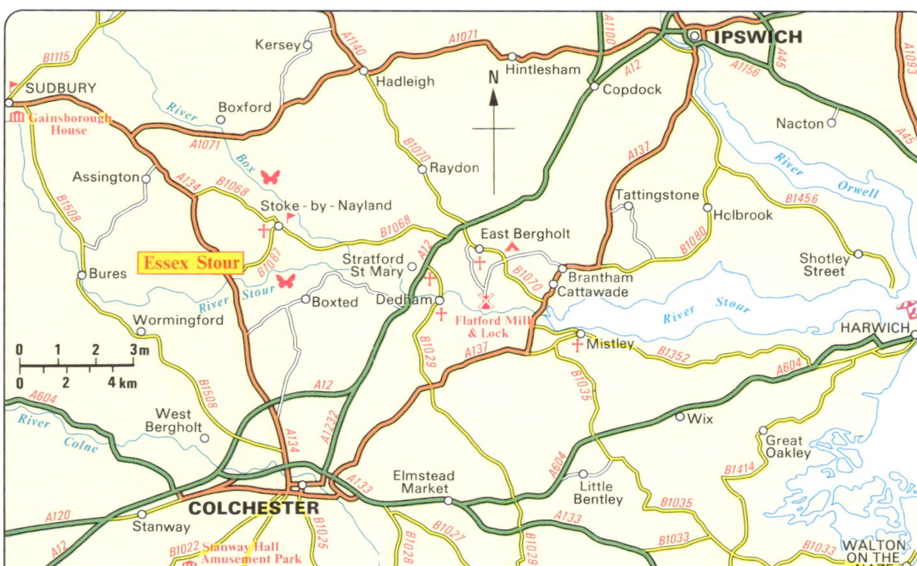

River Box
Good trout fishing, but visitors' chances limited and advance booking essential
Daily tickets: AWA, Essex River Division, 129 Springfield Road, Chelmsford

Harwich
Fine harbour fishing for ray and sole, plus conger, flatfish, tope and whiting by boat
Tackle shop: Sherwood Tackle, Dovercourt, Harwich

Upper Thames

Abingdon – Lechlade

Water Authority
Thames Water Authority – rod licence required and permits also issued for weir fishing
Tel: Reading (0734) 593333

Angling Associations
Coventry District Angling Association
Abingdon and Oxford Alliance
Oxford District Angling Association
Radcot Angling Preservation Club
London Anglers' Association

Tackle shops
G Williams, Headington, Oxford
Bait & Tackle, Oxford
A Smith, Oxford

Close Seasons
Salmon and trout: October 1 – March 31, *coarse fish:* March 15 – June 15

Rising to the east of the Cotswolds near Cirencester, the mighty River Thames meanders its way through a wide Oxfordshire valley, splits the Home Counties and, after a 210-mile course, enters the North Sea at Nore near Southend. During this long trip, the Thames changes its character many times. From a small brook running clear over the Cotswold chalk, it becomes the wide and powerful river that is a holiday attraction for hundreds of boat-borne leisure seekers. Despite the enormous industrial and treated sewage effluents and the tourist pressures it is subjected to, fish life in the river has managed to survive and flourish.

In fact the Thames is now cleaner than it has been for at least half a century – gross pollution is now considered to be confined only to those reaches below the London dock area. So confident is the Thames Water Authority in its clean-up programme, that in 1979 thousands of tiny salmon were introduced into the river's upper reaches in an attempt to once again restore the Thames as one of Britain's finest game rivers.

It will be several years before the success of this experiment is proven, but there are already signs that these King of fish can and will find their way past Tower Bridge. Already the brown trout is thriving in the many weir pools along the river, adding to the wide variety of coarse fish available.

From the angler's point of view, the section of the river from Abingdon up to Lechlade is now the most prominent and can give first-class sport. The river is controlled by the Thames Water Authority, who oversee boating interests as well as issue the required rod licence. A Thames Water permit is also required if you want access to the weirs, all of which hold considerable stocks of barbel, chub, bream, dace, carp, perch, pike and a few grayling (note the weirs are the quietest spots in peak periods). The major part of the angling here is controlled by angling clubs and local authority interests and access is very good for the visiting angler.

In Abingdon itself, the Abingdon Angling Association holds some rights, but it is the Borough Council that has the majority of the water. The council length covers about two and a half miles from Culham footbridge upstream to Nuneham Courtenay railway bridge. This includes a large weirpool which produces some excellent catches of barbel and chub. While the excellent angling around Abbey Meadow Island is reserved for residents, day and season tickets for the rest of the river are available to visitors.

Moving upstream towards Oxford, angling comes under the control of more local clubs such as the Oxford District Angling Association. This association holds the fishing at Sandford and around five miles from Osney Bridge which includes the notable Port

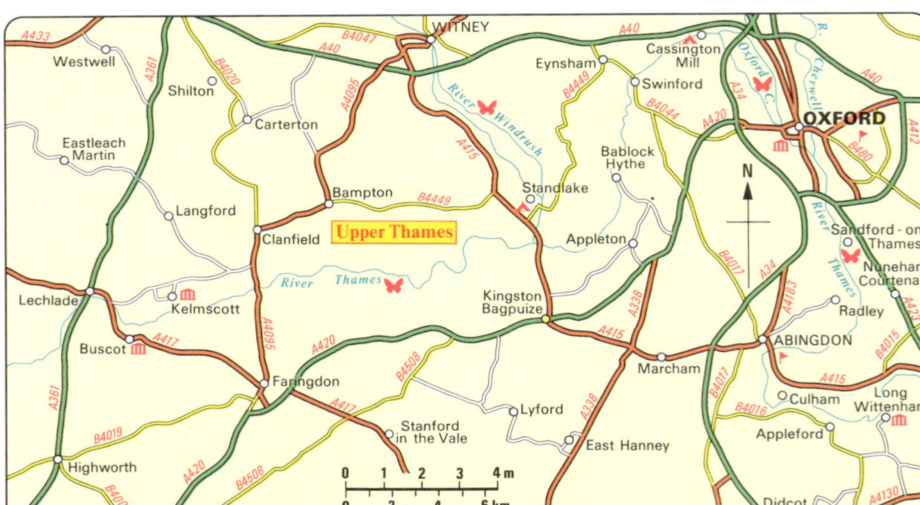

Oxford Canal
Coarse fishing for most species with good chances for the visitor
Daily tickets (Oxford – Kidlington): Waltonian Tackle, 30a Observatory Street, Oxford

Water Authority: as River Windrush

River Windrush
Good chub, dace and roach, but ticket fishing limited

Daily tickets: The Royal Oak, Burford or The Rose Revived, Newbridge
Water Authority: TWA
Tel: (0734) 593333

Camping
Eynsham: Cassington Mill Caravan Park ►►
Tel: (0865) 881081
Rural 83-pitch site 5m NW of Oxford
Open Apr–Oct, no bookings
Standlake: Standlake Caravans ►►
Tel: (086 731) 239
Level 50-pitch site 6m S of Witney off A415
Open Apr–Oct, must book Jul–Aug

Golfing
Abingdon: Frilford Heath:
Tel: (0865) 390428
Two courses with large greens, 18 holes, 6768yds (6006), par 72 (69), SSS73 (69)
Oxford: North Oxford:
Tel: (0865) 54924
Pleasant parkland course, 18 holes, 5805yds, par 67, SSS68
Southfield:
Tel: (0865) 42158
Good testing course, 18 holes, 6236yds, par 70, SSS70

Riding
Oxford: Oxford Riding School, Garsington
Tel: (086 736) 383

General
Buscot: Buscot Park: 18th-century house with notable water gardens
Open Apr–Sep (Wed, Thu & Fri) 2–6
Kelmscott: Manor House: gabled house, once home of William Morris
Open Apr–Sep (1st Wed in month)
Oxford: Ashmolean Museum of Art & Archaeology: vastly comprehensive museum, the oldest in England
Open all year daily 10–4 (Sun 2–4)
Tel: (0865) 57522
Oxford University: large complex of fine colleges, usually accessible
Rotunda Museum: impressive collection of dolls' houses c1700–1900
Open May–Sep 2–5 (Sun only)
Woodstock: Blenheim Palace: superb Vanbrugh mansion rich in Churchilliana
Open mid-Mar–Oct 11.30–5

Meadow section. Week and fortnight holiday permits are available and visitors should have very good sport with most of the main Thames species. Bream are the major catch here, although barbel, chub and roach make up the catch weight in most swims.

On the towpath side through Radley, it is the Oxford Alliance that takes up the rights although the Oxfordshire bank through Nuneham Park Estate is private fishing. The Alliance also holds some fishing at Swinford and Eynsham – but for access to Eynsham Weir, a favourite with local rods, get a Thames Water Authority permit.

Among a number of fisheries owned by riverside pubs and hotels, the 200-yard length run by the Ferry Inn at Bablock Hythe is a prominent barbel swim. This fast fighting fish is in the river in considerable numbers and from this particular area some of the best Thames barbel are reported every year. The Maybush Inn near Newbridge holds one and a half miles of river facing a bank controlled by the Rose Revived Inn. It is here that several stretches reserved for members of large Midlands angling clubs such as the Birmingham Angling Association and Coventry District Angling Association begin.

Upstream of these two fisheries, trout begin to be taken in increasing numbers. While occasional brown trout are taken in the Trout Inn stretch (there is a large car park here), it is around the Rushey weir that this sport becomes more prominent. Still in Oxfordshire, at Radcot, the local association sells tickets from headquarters at the Swan Inn. For two and a half miles of the river, barbel are a principal catch and there have been recent reports of trout up to 9lb in the Radcot weir pool.

The giant London Anglers' Association has gained much of the fishing around Lechlade itself but bankside bailiffs will sell day tickets. There is a Trout Inn here that really earns its name. Controlling two and a half miles of good mixed fishery available on day ticket, the Inn, at St John's lock, also issues special tickets for a small pool at a nearby bridge that holds a superb head of trout.

If, like many visitors, you and your family are travelling by riverboat on a cruising holiday from the many yards above and below Abingdon, much of the day takes care of itself in the rituals of boating. Do not miss the chance, however, to moor up in Oxford and explore this university city which dates back to the 8th-century. Among the many colleges, all of individual interest, Christ Church, founded by Cardinal Wolsey and with a bell tower by Christopher Wren, is of particular note. For rainy days Oxford has many enclosed sports facilities and a fine set of museums, including the Museum of Science History which has one of the world's finest collection of early scientific instruments.

Didcot is also within striking distance from the river at Appleford, just south of Abingdon. Once an important railway junction, Didcot is now the home of the Great Western Society's Railway Centre. The Society have assembled an enormous collection of engines and rolling stock from this historic railway and steam days are held on most Sundays and at Bank Holidays. Next door to Appleford is Long Wittenham, home of one of Britain's more curious collections. It is devoted to miniature scenes, showing British life in the Thirties and a scaled down railway wends to the sea through 'Madder Valley', a fictional, but realistic, region.

An alternative to holidays afloat is camping. One of the best sites in the area is by the riverside at Wallingford – council-run, the site has impressive facilities (including a nearby swimming pool) but you do need to book well in advance. Other sites are at Standlake and Cassington Mill near Oxford.

Walkers need tread no further than the river's towpath (and paths which parallel the water) to enjoy constantly changing sights, from marshy islands inhabited by many species of waterfowl, swans (although the famous Royal and Guild-owned swans are further downstream), and a constant procession of boats large and small. The downlands of Berkshire and Oxfordshire are of contrasting beauty and several long walks start out from the Abingdon area.

If you are not based afloat – and there is no more exciting way to see the river – many small boatyards are at the water's edge on the stretch from Abingdon to Oxford where craft can be hired by the hour or day. In Oxford itself the backwater of the Cherwell is a draw to summer punting parties viewing meadows and college grounds the lazy way. This is, after all, the scene which was the backdrop to that famous animal tale *Wind in the Willows* and the hilarious Jerome K Jerome adventures of *Three Men in a Boat*. It was Ratty, something of an angler himself, who said 'there's *nothing* – absolutely nothing – half so much worth doing as simply messing about in boats'.

The Norfolk Broads

The Broads are over 200 miles of navigable waterway in predominantly flat fenland offering extensive free coarse fishing from boats and some limited bank fishing (mainly on tidal stretches)

Water Authority
Anglian Water Authority, River Division
Tel: Norwich (0603) 615161

Principal Angling Club
Norwich & District Angling Association
Tel: (0603) 25682

Selected Boat Hire Centres
W Beale, The Straithe Garage, Hickling
Tel: (069 261) 280
Whispering Reeds Boatyard, Hickling
Tel: (069 261) 314
Barton Angler Hotel, Horning
Tel: (069 23) 740
E Burton & Sons, Wroxham
Tel: (060 53) 2751

Close Season
Coarse fish: March 15 – June 15

There can be no place in Britain that has so benefited from the environmental aftermath of man's industry as the Norfolk Broads. For this water and wildlife paradise covering nearly 200 square miles of the county is largely the result of 13th–16th-century peat digging and subsequent fen drainage schemes that have interlaced the rivers and broads with a fine pattern of drains and cuts. Industry continues to wreak change on the area, but now it is tourism that is the major threat to the revival of the Broads as one of Britain's foremost coarse fishing areas, having apparently survived the ravages of the algal poisoning *Prymnesium* during the Sixties. The beauty of the Broads is still that by road, footpath and, of course, by boat, it is still possible to find seclusion and rewarding angling along hundreds of miles of navigable waters.

The Broads system covers two distinct areas of the hinterland west of the holiday highspots of Great Yarmouth and Lowestoft. The southern Broads feed the rivers Yare and Waveney, both offering many excellent free fishing stretches for roach, bream, chub and the newly introduced predatory zander. But here we concentrate on the northern Broads which offer the more picturesque holiday locations and considerable fishing variety. These stretches of water, often set against a background of dense woodland, are feeders of the rivers Bure and Ant and the source of the Thurne. These are waters which suffered more than most from *Prymnesium*, but are now recovering to offer splendid sport to the holiday angler. It is probable that the fishing will be even better in a few years' time, provided the influx of tourists is not excessive.

Almost all the navigable Broads and rivers can be fished free of charge with an Anglian Water Authority licence, but bank fishing throughout the area is very limited. There is day ticket fly fishing on the upper reaches of the Bure (north west of Coltishall – apply to the AWA), but as the river becomes deeper and wider and reaches Wroxham it changes character. While fewer, but more consistently large, fish can be pulled out of the Aylsham–Wroxham stretch of the river, there are far more fish in the stretch from Wroxham–Horning. These are haunts of roach and bream, with pike in the winter months. 'Easy' fishing continues down river to Acle, thirteen miles away by water. Below Acle the current and tide (not to speak of the boat traffic) make it a lot more difficult, and real skill is required to make worthwhile catches from Acle to the Stracey Arms public house (on the main A47 Norwich–Yarmouth road).

Some of the best free fishing on this lazily tidal section of the Bure is the reach from the Ant mouth to half a mile past the Upton Dyke, a stretch which includes a mile of the Fleet Dyke, connecting the river to South Walsham Broad. This beautiful expanse of water consists of two distinct lakes – only the outer one can be fished free from boats.

Few visitors or anyone acquainted with small boating can have failed to hear the comic stories of boats passing under Potter Heigham Bridge. This mediaeval stone structure, taken under pilotage by larger hire boats, accounts for many boat masts every year. Peak holiday periods see long queues developing to pass through the narrow arch on the way up the Thurne to Hickling Broad, Meadow Dyke and Horsey Mere.

The whole of the Thurne teems with roach and bream, and its five-mile length (all tidal) offers challenging all-season angling. Winter brings big shoals of roach and bream out of the shallow broads which are the river's source, but with its easy access for bank fishing and completely free boat fishing it draws the summer crowds, too. Hickling Broad is the largest in Norfolk and its tragedy is the extinction of the enormous pike inhabiting the shallow waters during the algal poisoning crisis. Happily fish are on the way back here, and bream of over 3lb, roach of about a 1lb and pike up to 20lb are again becoming the norm. Heigham Sound and the interconnecting White Slea offer similar possibilities. Horsey Mere, a triangular patch of National Trust-owned water deep in reed beds, was once Britain's finest pike lake. The 40lb monsters of the late Fifties have been replaced by a growing population of smaller fish and some parallel increases in the roach and bream shoals. Day tickets are required, available from Hall Cottage and Staithe Store by the village moorings (there is limited bank fishing here, too).

Pike fishing on Ormsby Broad

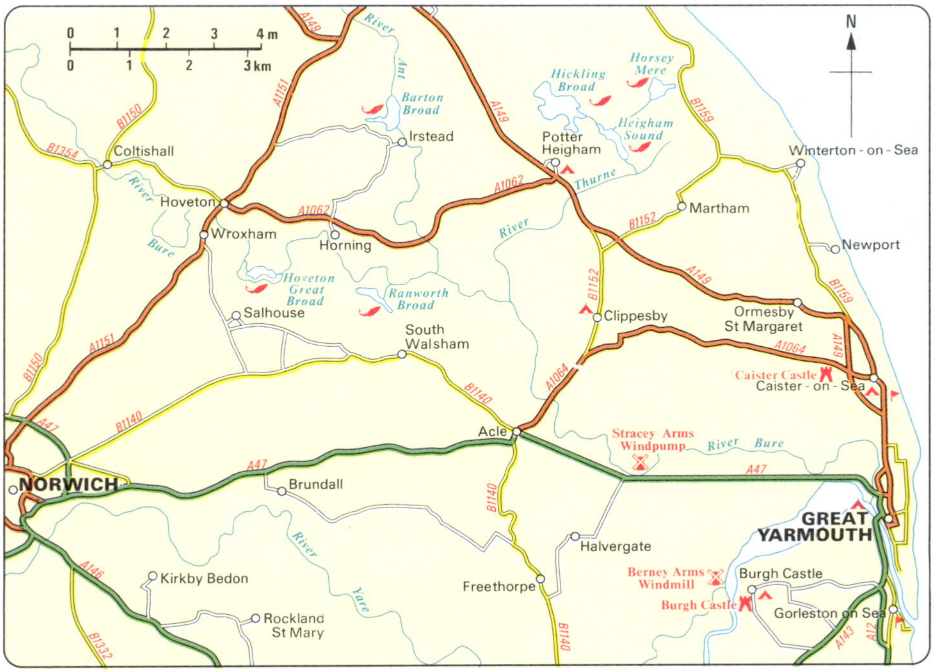

Boat traffic interferes with fishing on the River Ant. This narrow and relatively shallow river is little more than a stream until it becomes canalised near Honing and then enters the fenland just north of Barton Broad. Barton has the distinction of being the only large broad through which a river flows – boat traffic usually sticks to the main channel, leaving the lake's margins to the angler. Here, and in the remaining five-mile stretch of the Ant, down to its junction with the Bure, near the ruins of St Benet's Abbey, is a chance for the elusive rudd. Between Irstead Village and the Bure are free fishing reaches and day ticket stretches controlled by Norwich Angling Association (Ludham Bridge to the Ant mouth).

Lining the Bure from just above Wroxham, Broadland's boating Mecca, to just past the Ant junction, are the broads lying within a comfortable day's boating from the yards of Wroxham and Horning. Ranworth (or Malthouse) Broad is, like South Walsham, in two parts – the outer section is free fishing but the inner is controlled by Norwich Angling Association, and day tickets are issued only from June 16th–September 30th and March 1st–14th. Similar restrictions apply to the Decoy Broad, which is a nature reserve and inaccessible to motor boats. Salhouse Great and Little Broads are fishable by day ticket from bailiffs and this very pretty double lake system also has some bank fishing accessible by road from Salhouse village.

Hoveton Great Broad forms one of the many private nature reserves in the Broadland system and although it cannot be fished by visitors, it is well worth a visit for the one-mile nature trail (boat access only) displaying fenland flora and fauna in a particularly wild and undisturbed environment. Avoid Wroxham Broad at weekends as it is the haunt of crowds of small-boaters – weekdays are a more enjoyable and fruitful time to enjoy the free fishing here and the peace is satisfying.

There is only one way to really explore the Broads and that is by boat. A week or fortnight's holiday on board a motor or sailing boat hired from Wroxham or Horning allows plenty of time for exploration of the northern part of the system and a sample of delights such as waterside pubs (many with facilities for children), trips round the nature trails surrounding Hickling Broad, walks to the coast at Horsey and Winterton and visits to restored Broadland drainage windmills (like the picturesque one at Stracey Arms).

The coast from Winterton, south to Lowestoft, is a major holiday complex with good beaches and all the usual fun-of-the-fair family attractions. Yarmouth is as good a centre for Broads exploration by car (and day boat hire) as Wroxham and has many tourist attractions in the immediate area. Examples are the Caister Castle and Car Museum and the Fritton Lake Pleasure Park (actually a broad with boating, fishing, putting and a variety of other family pursuits).

The Norfolk Wildlife Park is well worth a trip away from the Broads for a day. This zoological park of fifty acres houses one of Europe's largest collections of mammals and birds in conditions as close as possible to their natural habitats. Specially built aviaries enable visitors to observe bird behaviour, and a particular attraction is a collection of rare ornamental pheasants. The park, well-signposted from the A1067 Norwich–Hunstanton road (about ten miles from Norwich), is open to the public throughout the year.

Camping
Burgh Castle: Cherry Farm Caravan & Chalet Park ►►► Mill Road *Tel: (0493) 780229*, Orchard and grassland site with 105 pitches, 4m from sea and a stone's throw from Burgh Castle ruins and Breydon Water Open Jun–mid-Sep
Caister-on-Sea: Grasmere Caravan Park ►►► 7 Bultitudes Lake, Yarmouth Road *Tel: (0493) 720382* 49-pitch grass and gravel site for caravans only on A149 Open Apr–mid-Oct
Clippesby: Clippesby Holiday Caravan Park ►►► *Tel: (049 377) 367* Grassy 60-pitch side in woodland off B1152 – close to Thurne and Bure Open mid-May–Sep
Great Yarmouth: Vauxhall Holiday Park ►►►►► *Tel: (0493) 57231* Full facilities, site close to town, Breydon Water and sea with 435 pitches Open late May–late Sep, no bookings accepted
Potter Heigham: Homestead Site ►►► Bridge Road, Potter Heigham *Tel: (069 27) 461* 10-pitch grass and gravel site on bank of Thurne off A149 Open Apr–Oct, booking essential

Cycle Hire
Norwich: Dodgers, 69 Trinity Street *Tel: (0603) 22499*
Scott Cruiser Ltd (Rent a Bike) *Tel: (0603) 713948*

Golfing
Gorleston: Warren Road, Gorleston, Gt Yarmouth *Tel: (0493) 61082* 3m from Gt Yarmouth off A12, 18 holes, 5950yds, par 70, SSS68
Gt Yarmouth and Caister: Beach House, Caister *Tel: (0493) 728699* 2m north of Gt Yarmouth on A149. Renowned competition course, 18 holes, 6254yds, par 70, SSS70

Major Boat Hire Operators
Lowestoft: Hoseasons Holidays, Sunway House *Tel: (0502) 62181*
Norwich: Broads Charters Ltd, Old School House, Ringland *Tel: (0603) 868702*
Wroxham: Blakes Holidays *Tel: (060 53) 3225*

Walking Trails
Hickling Broad Water Trail (escorted boats) – contact Warden's Office, Stubb Road, Hickling *Tel: (069 261) 276*
Hoveton Great Broad, Contact Regional Officer, Nature Conservancy Council, 69 Bracondale, Norwich *Tel: (0603) 20558*

Grafham Water

Water Authority
Anglian Water Authority – Great Ouse River Division or regional rod licence required
Tel: (0480) 56181

Reservations
Area Manager's Office, Grafham Water Area, West Parry, Huntingdon, Cambridgeshire
Tel: (0480) 810247
Day, evening, weekly tickets available – motor and rowing boats for hire.
Enquiries also to Fishing Lodge
Tel: (0480) 810531

Close Season
Varies, but generally closed from end of October – late April

Catch record
Brown trout: 12lb 5oz

Grafham Water first opened its gates to trout fishermen in 1966 and since those early days this Cambridgeshire reservoir has become one of the best known stillwater fisheries in Britain. In fact Grafham is considered by many to be where the trout fishing revolution really started.

Camping
Grafham: Old Manor Caravan Park ►►►
Tel: (0480) 810264
Well-kept 66-pitch site
Open all year, must book
Huntingdon: Anchor Cottage Riverside Caravan & Camping Site ►►
Tel: (0480) 55642
29-pitch woodland site
Open all year, must book Jul–Aug
Hemingford Abbots: Heming Abbots Caravan Park ►►►
Flat, 20-pitch site off A604
Open Apr–Oct, no bookings
Thrapston: Mill Marina Caravan & Boat Park ►
Tel: (080 12) 2850
Grassy, 41-pitch site with river access
Open Apr–Sep, must book public holidays

Golfing
St Ives:
Tel: (0480) 64459
Scenic parkland course, 18 holes, 6052yds, par 68, SSS69
St Neots:
Tel: (0480) 72363
Parkland course with easy walking, 18 holes, 5686yds, par 68, SSS67

Sailing
Grafham Water Sailing Club
Tel: (0480) 810478

Walking Trails
Monks Wood: a 375-acre nature reserve noted for rare plants. Turn right off A1, 3m N of Alconbury

General
Brampton: Pepys' House: the famous diarist's gabled cottage
Open all year (ex Sun) by appointment only
Tel: (0480) 53431
Buckden: Buckden Palace: ancient Tudor palace off A1, 6m N of St Neots
Open Jul–Sep (Sun only) 3–7
Huntingdon: Cromwell Museum: restored Norman building with Cromwellian collection
Open all year (ex Mon) times vary
Tel: (0480) 52181
Hinchingbrooke House: Tudor mansion incorporating mediaeval nunnery
Open Easter then Mar–Jul (Sun only) 2–5
St Ives: Morris Museum: local books, MSS & artefacts
Open all year (ex Mon) times vary
Tel: (0480) 65101

Under the control of the Anglian Water Authority's Great Ouse Division, the 1600-acre fishery is renowned for the big brown trout which thrive on rich feeding provided by vast shoals of coarse fish. Although Grafham is retained solely as a trout fishery, the Anglian Water Authority regularly nets huge hauls of prime roach, bream and pike for restocking other waters.

Fishing is allowed from both bank and boat, but unlike many of the bigger waters, this one sees big fish taken from the shore with surprising regularity. Some measure of the catch rate at Grafham can be drawn from figures for the 1978 season when a record 36 710 trout were landed. Among the best fishes of that immense bag were a brown trout of 9lb 2oz and a rainbow of 6lb 4oz, both taken from the shore. Brown trout taken by boat are usually over 10lb.

Few of the fish are actually put in the water at anywhere near that size. They grow fast by drinking in the rich soup of *Daphnia* in the water. This can stimulate a small stock fish to grow up to $1\frac{1}{2}$lb within less than two summer months.

Anglers can cash-in on the fish's *Daphnia* feeding sprees by playing the gaudier lures, such as Whisky Fly, Mickey Finn or the bright green Leprechaun. On brighter days the hordes of minute *Daphnia* sink nearer the bottom and anglers need to use sinking lines to place the lures nearer to the prey. Dull days bring both the food and the trout nearer the surface and a fast stripped lure on a floating line should provide stirring action.

Select your spot on the bank with care as weed growths in Grafham can be dense and in some parts this makes bank fishing extremely difficult. Check with the fishing lodge about those sections of the bank which may be closed from July 15th until the end of September due to excessive weed growth.

It is at Grafham's vast concrete dam that bank fishing really pays. The water is deep within easy casting range and the bigger fish come in close to hunt for fry. A big white lure resembling a young bream can pay dividends and attract really big trout.

Afloat, Grafham has even greater potential and many of the techniques that characterise modern stillwater fishing were first expounded here to combat the depth of the water and the wind currents to which this wide expanse of water is exposed.

Heavy lead-cored lines trolled through the depths with big tandem lures will search out the larger brown trout. But for real action, a white tandem muddler pulled back through the waves to make a wake brings browns and rainbows dashing right up to the side of the boat. During the August hatch of sedge flies, trout can be seen mopping up enormous numbers in the Water's sheltered bays. An imitation of the adult fly (or the nymph) cast on a floating line is a good bet and among the best locations for this more traditional sport are the bays at the western end near Savages Creek.

Towards the end of the season Grafham experiences yet another change of mood as the stock is overtaken by the urge to spawn. These last few weeks see some of the best fishing as the bigger trout turn to fry-feeding in preparation for the rigours of breeding. They will hit a big lure with great speed, so it is as well to be prepared for some demanding sport.

This completion of the season's cycle is one of Grafham's great attractions – even for the regular visitor it provides superb variety. For the novice it is an ideal proving ground for the basic techniques, indeed a number of beginners' courses are held here throughout the season; they are organised by the fishery warden.

Grafham's popularity as a family leisure venue is in part due to the very wide open spaces around the banks, ideal for picnicking families. Close to the water is an excellent campsite – Old Manor Caravan Park – which is open all year round for holidaying or weekend visits. The site is six and a half acres of level grass and woodlands with a wide range of facilities which include a heated swimming pool, a children's playground and a shop for basic food requirements. Many of the sixty-six individually bookable pitches have mains electricity supplies for an all-comforts stay. The park is very popular, so it is always advisable to book in advance.

The reservoir is also one of the country's foremost inland sailing centres which hosts many class championships, Olympic trials and international events during the May to Autumn period. Day and weekly sailing can be arranged and there are plans to run short sailing courses from the club.

While Grafham itself is home to hundreds of waterfowl, there are more exotic species to be seen at the Lodge Reserve, headquarters of the Royal Society for the Protection of Birds. The Reserve and nearby Sutton Fen total over a hundred acres of protected habitat – visitors can walk the nature trail in the grounds and see a splendid exhibition of the Society's ornithological work.

Only four miles on from Sandy are airborne fascinations of a strictly man-made kind. Old Warden airfield is the site of the famous Shuttleworth Collection of Vintage Cars and Historic Aeroplanes. While the majority of the aircraft (and many other curios of early road and air transport) are in static displays, weekends from May to September see a small swarm of them in the air.

This is a part of the country with a wealth of historical associations. Grafham itself appears in the Doomsday Book and the Manor (once standing close to where the campsite is now landscaped), was just one of Oliver Cromwell's homes. Samuel Pepys' parents lived at nearby Brampton and it was here that he buried a fortune when in fear of a Dutch invasion. The house can be viewed by appointment. The gabled cottage is worth the effort.

Combine a view of history with something to keep active and inquiring children amused in a visit to Lilford Park. This 240-acre adventure land on the A605 between Oundle and Thrapston is centred on a 17th-century Jacobean mansion (open to view at certain times). In the grounds are extensive aviaries, a children's farm offering pony rides and face-to-face encounters with animals, a crafts museum and collection, and a 'Jungleland' adventure playground. An antiques and crafts market is held here and there is a motor show during the Spring Bank holiday.

Huntingdon includes a number of attractions such as Hinchingbrooke House, a Tudor Mansion which boasts a mediaeval nunnery. There is also a Cromwell museum.

Plan your trip to Grafham as far in advance as possible – a month ahead will ensure that you can get the days you want and that a boat will be available. About 70 000 fish have been put into the water during 1980 alone, so even the most inexperienced anglers stand a chance of a big catch – and a very eatable one at that.

With expertise an angler may catch enough to feed a holidaying family.

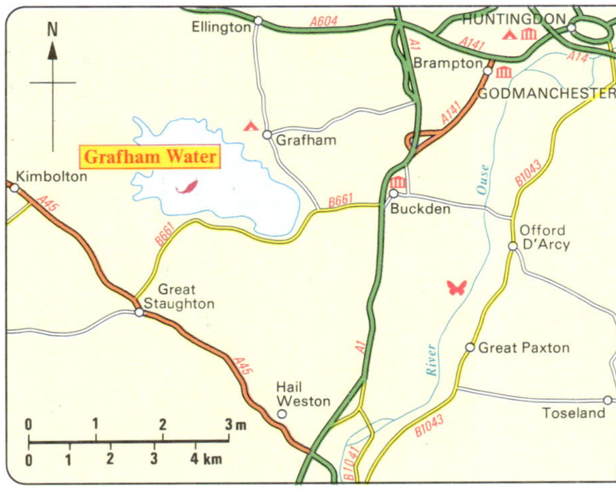

River (Great) Ouse
Most freshwater species may be landed, especially barbel and chub
Daily tickets: from bank or keeper for Huntingdon, Offord, St Neots
Daily tickets in advance:
Golden Lion, St Ives
Tel: (0480) 63159
Godmanchester, from bank or keeper
St Ives and District Fish Preservation and Angling Society (D Denton), 49 Little Farthing Close, St Ives
St Neots and District Angling Society (S E Smith), 10 River Terrace, St Neots
Tel: (0480) 75995
Water Authority: AWA, Diploma House, Grammar School Walk, Huntingdon, Cambridgeshire
Tel: (0480) 56181

A reservoir Rainbow Trout

Billing Aquadrome

Water Authority
Anglian Water Authority – Welland and Nene River Division licence required
Tel: (0480) 56181

Reservations
Billing Aquadrome Ltd, Little Billing, Northampton
Tel: (0604) 408181
Day, night, weekly and season tickets available

Close Seasons
Varies, but is usually from close of park in mid-October until June 16. River Nene: *trout:* September 29 – February 28/29; *pike:* March 15 – September 30; all other fish: March 14 – June 16 (Note: live baits of over 20cm must not be used.)

Catch record
Carp: 42lb 4oz

In the heart of the Northamptonshire countryside, lush, rolling grassland, rivers and many small lakes, lies a nationally famed carp fishing water which is almost incongruously set in a 270-acre family amusement park. Billing Aquadrome, established in 1932 on riverside land surrounding old gravel workings, is just three miles east of Northampton off the A45 at Great Billing. Within the grounds are ten fishable lakes, facilities on a one and a half mile stretch of River Nene bank, a boating marina with access to the river, a full facilities campsite with the top AA 5-pennant rating, and a set of entertainments that should exhaust the most active of families.

Billing's reputation as a carp water was founded in the early Sixties when local angler Bob Reynolds landed a 33lb 2oz mirror carp. His bait? – a piece of banana. Since then, techniques have improved, to bring in many large catches of carp including a bag of 135lb of fish in one week by the same angler. It was in the Sixties, too, that Ray Clay took the lakes' record with an amazing 42lb 4oz fish which is still, today, the third largest mirror carp landed in Britain.

Sad to relate, however, the water is unlikely ever to yield carp of this size again. While good fish are still hauled in here it seems the large specimens have declined in favour of healthy stocks of bream. Good six and seven pound bream are a regular feature of catches which can amount to several hundredweight of fish at a sitting. Tench, roach and eels are here in great numbers, too, so whatever your favourite technique, the sport can be exhilarating. The good news for carp specialists, however, is that some 2 000 good-sized fish were introduced into the five main lakes during 1979 and catches are on the way up again.

Like many gravel pits, the Billing lakes are fairly shallow, with ridge and furrow bottoms, some lakes having islands and sand bars. The fishing is generally very easy, with little weed growth to contend with and good banks to sit on. Tench and roach tend to be taken at the lake margins by float fishermen with maggot bait. Carp are taken by ledgering the middle waters with maggot worm or any of the more specialised carp baits. Bream at Billing are not at all selective and seem to take almost any bait offered. It is not at all unusual for carp men to take the bigger bream.

The pressure of crowds enjoying the park's other attractions is the biggest drawback to serious fishing at Billing. The biggest fish are in Willow Lake, which is the main boating pool and is surrounded by bars, the cafeteria and the miniature train ride. The park is, however, open twenty-four hours and it is quite possible to avoid the crowds by night and early morning fishing. The best of all worlds is enjoyed by the angler who is actually camping in the park's own site. With some waters literally at the tent door it is possible to bait up a swim last thing at night and then hit into a good head of bream at dawn with several hours to go before the banks are disturbed by non-angling visitors.

If you do want to fish the day through, the eight lakes furthest from the main attractions are the best bet. There is good tree cover ideal for stalking the sensitive tench.

The Nene itself is an extremely important coarse fishing river which is a favourite of anglers from the Midlands and East Anglia. Large sections of the river are controlled by local associations, but the majority offer day ticket facilities to visitors or have few membership restrictions and can be joined quite cheaply. Good clubs to contact are the Northampton and Nene Angling Club, Kettering, Thrapston and District Angling Association and the Leicester Amalgamated.

In the middle waters of the river, chub can be caught, and the river has been stocked with barbel in common with many keenly-fished streams. These particular fish have proved rather elusive over the last few years but they do occasionally feature in catches. Most anglers use maggot baits, but chub can be lured with cheese and lugworms are useful to get the larger eels.

The angler can rest assured that if he takes a family to Billing they are unlikely to run out of things to do. Even if you do not take your own boat (rowing boats, canoes and unpowered inflatables can be launched on the lakes and the river for a small charge), there are rowing boats for hire on Willow Lake. For walkers, just to inspect the park will while away an hour or so. There is also the fairground. Improvements are being made all the time, but the central attractions remain the fast-moving action of features such as the Astro-Glide and Luna Jets. You can even explore the park by four-seater family tricycle.

One of the earliest features of the Aquadrome was the fully-restored corn mill, one of the many 18th- and 19th-century watermills in the area. The mill is a museum displaying many aspects of this local industry. For the more active visitors there is a very large open air swimming pool close to the boating lake.

Camping
Olney: Emberton Park ►►►
Tel: (0234) 711575
Pleasant 56-pitch site
Open Apr–Oct, must book Jul–Aug

Golfing
Northampton: Delapre Complex:
Tel: (0604) 64036
Large golf complex including 9 holes, par 3 course, pitch & putt, 18 holes, 6403yds, par 71, SSS71
Kingsthorpe:
Tel: (0604) 711173
Good parkland course, 18 holes, 6000yds, par 69, SSS68
Northampton:
Tel: (0604) 711054
Parkland course with easy walking, 18 holes, 5369yds, par 70, SSS72

Riding
Brampton Stables, Manor Farm, Church Brampton, Northamptonshire
Tel: (0604) 842051

Walking Trails
Lings Wood Nature Trail: 1m (1hr) signposted circular trail. Start at Billing Lings bus stop, 4m NE of Northampton on A45

General
Althorp: 16th-century home of Spencer family, fine china collection
Open mid-Apr–Sep (Tue, Thu, Sun), plus daily in Aug (ex Mon)
Castle Ashby: Castle Ashby House: finely furnished 17th-century mansion, home of the Marquess of Northampton
Open Easter then Jul–Aug daily 2–5
Tel: (060 129) 332
Northampton: Abington Park: large park & gardens with many sports facilities
Open all year (ex Sun, Oct–Mar)
Delapre Abbey: Northamptonshire public records office, in house built on site of ancient nunnery
Open all year
Olney: Cowper & Newton Museum: many manuscripts and personal effects of the poet William Cowper
Open Easter–Oct (ex Sun & Mon), plus Nov–Easter 2–5 only
Tel: (0234) 711516

Campers get a very good deal. In addition to the high level of facilities, which include a choice of five distinct areas of pitches, numerous water standpipes, and impressive toilet and shower blocks, many of the Aquadrome's main attractions are free to residents – including the superb fishing.

Wherever you go outside the Aquadrome gates you are never far from water, it seems. Just ten miles from Billing is that once-important artery, the Grand Union Canal. At Stoke Bruerne, embarkation point for many people's holidays afloat in restored waterways boats, is the Waterways Museum which traces the history of this canal and the many facets of the bargee's life. In this attractive basin at the waterside is another corn mill and a typical canalside pub.

If you can urge the family to venture there after Billing, there is another five-lake fishery in and around the grounds of the home of the Marquess of Northampton at Castle Ashby. The hall itself dates back to 1574 with a frontage by Inigo Jones of about 1635. The interior of the hall has many fine paintings and period furnishings.

There is history of a different kind at Purlieu Farm near Naseby. Sited on the battlefield of 1645, where Cromwell's Parliamentarians first turned the tide of Civil War against Charles I, the farm is a museum of the battle with sound commentaries on tactics played over a model battlefield and many artefacts from the slaughter that have been unearthed in the fields. The location also delves into the history of mechanised agriculture with a comprehensive collection of fine old tractors and implements.

While there is a lot of birdlife to be viewed at the Aquadrome, it is not so exotic as the 200 or so species on view at Weston Underwood Flamingo Gardens and Zoo where over 1 000 birds vie with a large mammal collection for attention. If the children's appetite for animals is still not sated, Guilsborough Grange Bird and Pet Park offers pony rides through parkland surrounding a distinctive 19th-century country house, now a reserve for birds, waterfowl and animals in near-natural habitats.

Return to Billing in the evening (in time to ground-bait your swim) and the chances are that the Willow Tree bar restaurant will be in full swing with free cabaret entertainment.

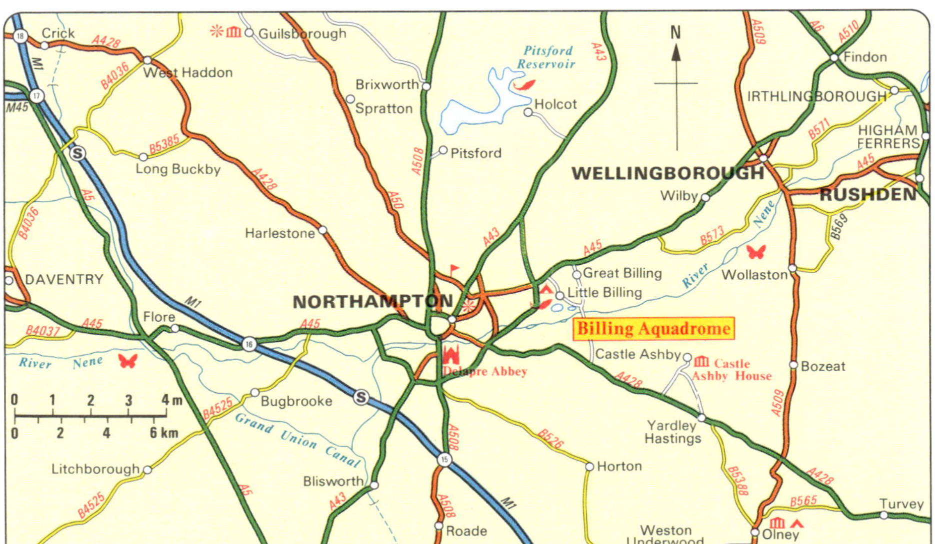

River Nene
Good coarse fishing especially bream & roach
Daily tickets (Northampton – Doddington): on bank or The Angling Centre, 88 St Leonard's Road, Northampton
Tel: (0604) 64847
Water Authority: AWA

Pitsford Reservoir
Well-stocked 700-acre trout fishery, 6m N of Northampton off A508
Daily tickets (Apr–Sep): AWA, Cliftonville, Northampton

Rutland Water

Water Authority
Anglian Water Authority – rod licence required, on sale with day and evening (after 5pm) tickets at Whitwell Lodge from 5.30am
Anglian Water Authority (Welland & Nene Division) North Street, Oundle
Tel: (083 22) 3701

Reservations
The Reservoir Manager, Rutland Water, Whitwell, Oakham, Leicestershire
Tel: Empingham (078 086) 770

Close Season
Varies but is generally from end October to April 25

Catch records
Best *rainbow trout* 1979 – 8lb 13oz
Best *brown trout* 1979 – 7lb 7oz

Rutland Water, the largest man-made water in Europe is fast making a name as one of the finest trout fisheries in Britain. With 3 100 acres of water to fish there is plenty of scope for the visiting angler who will find day tickets easily obtainable.

The reservoir (once called Empingham) is controlled by the Anglian Water Authority and in particular, the Welland and Nene Division, whose headquarters are at Oundle. The water covers a very large chunk of what was once the smallest county in Britain, Rutland.

Camping
Stamford: Casterton Filling Station & Motel ►►►
Tel: (0780) 54376
Flat 45-pitch site, 3m NW of Stamford off B1081
Open all year, must book Jul–Aug

Golfing
Luffenham Heath:
Tel: (0780) 720205
Rolling heathland course midway between Uppingham & Stamford, 18 holes, 6382yds, par 71, SSS70
Stamford: Burghley Park:
Tel: (0780) 2100
Short parkland course with fine greens, 18 holes, 5888yds, par 70, SSS68

Walking Trails
Belton Park Nature Trail: 1½m (1hr) signposted circular walk. Start from Belton House, Belton 3m N of Grantham off A607

General
Market Deeping: Rectory: 14th-century parsonage said to be oldest still inhabited in England
Open daily 11 onwards
Tel: (0778) 342237
Melton Mowbray: Melton Carnegie Museum: new collection depicting local life
Open all year 10–5 (Sun 2–5)
Tel: (0664) 69946
Stapleford Park: mansion & grounds with miniature steam railway, picnic area, garden centre – 5m E of Melton Mowbray off B676
Open Apr–Sep times vary
Tel: (057 284) 229/245
Oakham: Oakham Castle: old fortress with fine Norman hall & unique horseshoe collection
Open all year (Sun & Mon) afternoons only
Tel: (0572) 3654
Stamford: Brewery Museum: newly-opened (licensed!) museum
For opening times
Tel: (0780) 52186
Burghley House: England's finest Elizabethan house, with vast art collection – 1½m S of Stamford off B1081

Now merged with Leicestershire for administrative purposes, the county name lives on at this lake which is near the former county town of Oakham.

Angling is permitted from both boat and bank, although there are just a few parts of the shoreline set aside as nature reserves where no fishing is allowed. Some twenty-four miles of lake perimeter and the water's five-mile length mean that you will rarely be in a crowd – there are so many exciting bays, a tremendous variety of conditions and perfect fishing positions regardless of the weather or wind direction.

At the western end of the lake, the giant dam spans three-quarters of a mile and figures as one of the more popular spots to hunt the reservoir's hard-fighting rainbow and brown trout. Fishing at this end is not easy – the dam is high and the rough rock construction is no place for cowards. Then again, the rewards for patience are high.

There is more relaxing fishing to be had on the gently sloping banks around the rest of the U-shaped lake. For boat fishing Rutland has a fleet of sixty well-equipped craft – book well in advance at the fishing lodge (open from 5.30am for day tickets – 8.30am for boats) as demand is high. Fishing is by fly only but trolling of lures is allowed in one small section towards the dam end of the water. This method often brings home the most powerful brown trout. These are fish that have grown close to double figures in weight since the first stocks were introduced prior to the opening of the lake in 1977.

If you do take out a boat, do not rush out into the expanse of water without pausing to see the tame trout living near the moorings. These are real showmen and rise readily to the bailiff's handful of food.

Once out on the water or at your chosen bank spot, there is a choice of fishing for brown or rainbow trout plus the possible excitement of hooking a spectacular North American

Trout fishing on Rutland Water

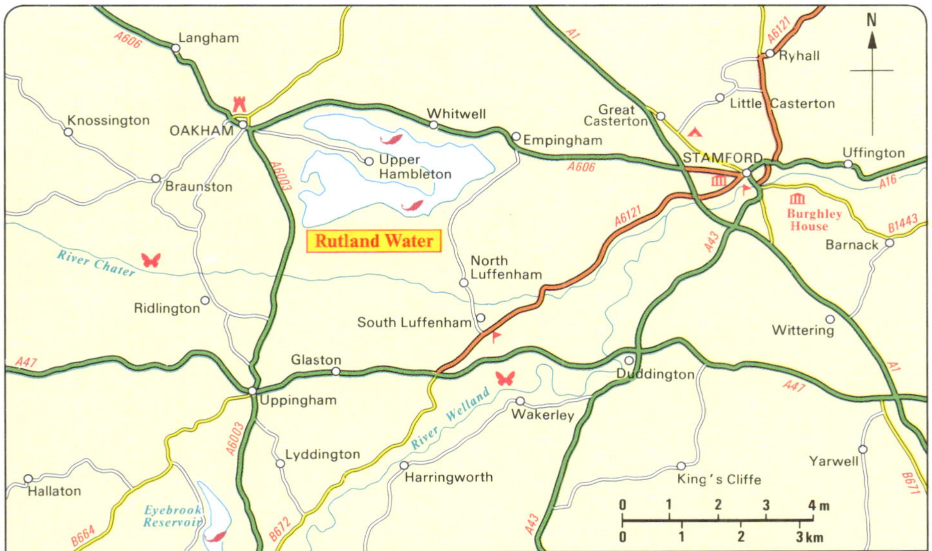

River Chater
Good dace and roach, but only by club membership
Daily tickets: The Golden Ball, Spalding or AWA, North Street, Oundle (riparian owner)
Club: Spalding Fishing Club
Water Authority: AWA
Tel: (0480) 56181

Eyebrook Reservoir
Well-stocked trout fishery, 3m S of Uppingham off A6003
Daily tickets (in advance): Corby District Water Co
Tel: (053 670) 264 or at Fishing Lodge during season (Apr–Sep)
Water Authority: as River Chater

River Welland
Fine chub, dace and roach
Daily tickets (Ketton-Stamford): Stamford-Welland Angling Association (free fishing through Stamford)
Water Authority: as River Chater

Brook trout. Eight thousand of these reputedly tough and fast-growing brutes were introduced to Rutland during 1980. The Anglian Water Authority normally stocks the water only with rainbow and brown trout – several thousand fish a season are released into the lake.

Early season tactics to tackle these fish are to try black or white lures fished slowly on sinking lines. A Black Chenille or a Sweeney Todd can be switched for a white lure such as White Chenille, Appetiser or Baby Doll. Later in the season, which starts around the beginning of May (the date varies each year), there is a hatch of large buzzers or midges. When these can be seen, a team of nymphs, such as a Pheasant Tail on the point or Green and Black Buzzers on two droppers, is well worth a try. Fish them slowly on a floating line, allowing the wind to develop a bow in the line, so pulling the flies around in an attractive arc.

On a vast water like Rutland, different locations are constantly turning up bumper catches, but even the first-time visitor can locate fish quickly. The secret is to drive around until you spot a bunch of anglers fishing together, the chances are that they are there because the location is currently on form. There are, of course, some favourite spots. Whitwell Creek, Sailing Club Bay, Barnsdale Creek and Hambleton Peninsula all have their share of fish. They are similar in having deep water within casting distance. Some of the best stands are where bushes or an old fence tumble over the bank into the water to create shade and camouflage for the fish.

Never use very fine tackle at Rutland. Leaders of 5lb are about the minimum breaking strain that can be used in safety. Rutland fish have a lot of swimming space and know how to use every inch of a long run.

If you do strike lucky, a day ticket at Rutland allows you to catch eight fish (and keep them!) – really lucky anglers will purchase additional tickets at the lodge during the day. After 5pm there are cheaper three-fish limit tickets available.

Beyond the lake's shore is the rest of the beautiful area of Rutland. It is hunting country of stately homes, rich grazing and small unspoilt villages. Oakham, a few miles to the west of the lake is a charming old regional centre. Just outside is the village of Langham, home, to real ale fans, of the Ruddles family brewery, one of Oakham's largest businesses. Oakham Castle has a unique collection of horseshoes in its Norman Hall. Legend has it that the majority of the shoes are ornamental tributes to the lordly owners from visiting royalty.

Stamford is the other nearby town. Built on the A1, which is at this stage on the line of the Roman Ermine Street, the town is centred round a cluster of small-scale stone-built houses and no fewer than five ancient churches. In the graveyard of St Martins is the tomb of famous fatty Daniel Lambert, who weighed in at 53 stone upon his death. Stamford's local brewery closed in 1974 and the building has become a museum to the craft. Burghley House, cradle of the powerful families of Cecil and Exeter, is on the outskirts of the town. Said to be one of England's finest Elizabethan homes, the house contains ornate ceilings, superb fireplaces and a very large collection of Italian old masters. Reflecting this area's long-forged links with the hunting, shooting and, of course, fishing fraternity, Burghley is the location for many horse trials, including the September three-day event.

Through Stamford on the B1443 is the Peakirk Wildfowl Trust reserve which has over 600 ducks, geese and swans of about 100 species in the nearly natural habitat of a water garden.

If you like collecting souvenirs of weekend and holiday visits to the heart of the country, there are none more flavoursome than the Stilton cheeses, pork pies and Hunt cake (fruit cake laced with rum) to be found in the shops of Melton Mowbray. From this bustling market town, walks are set out along the banks of the River Eye. Four miles out of town on the B676 is Stapleford Park, the grounds of a mansion with a miniature steam passenger railway, models of the liners SS *Northern Star* and *Southern Cross*, a lion reserve and picnic areas.

There is really no need to stray much further than the banks of this man-made water of Rutland to enjoy bluebell-carpeted woods, wild-life and well-signed walks. Maps of the water and the surrounding country are on sale at the fishing lodge at Whitwell Creek just off the A606 between Empingham and Oakham.

River Trent

Newark – Nottingham

Water Authority
Severn-Trent Water Authority
Trout and freshwater fish licence issued for annual and 28-day periods. Licences from many local dealers. Information on River Trent from: Area Recreation Officer, Severn-Trent Water Authority, Meadow Lane, Nottingham
Tel: (0602) 865007

Angling Associations
Midland Angling Association
Newark and District Piscatorial Federation
Nottingham Angling Association
Nottingham and District Federation of Angling Societies
Nottingham Piscatorial Society

Tackle Shops
The Tackle Box, Pavilion Road, Trent Bridge, Nottingham
Archie Tizeley, 100 Bunbury Street, Meadows, Nottingham
Walkers of Trowell, Nottingham Road, Trowell, Nottinghamshire
Tom Watson, 1 Oak Street, Carrington, Nottingham

Close Season
Coarse fish: March 15 – June 15

Since the turn of the century, the 170-mile River Trent was the dumping ground for all the filth of the north and east Midlands. From Stoke-on-Trent, Burton, Nottingham and Newark flowed massive loads of sewage and industrial effluent that all but killed the river's massive fish stocks. That most sensitive indicator of all, the salmon, was taken in thousands in the late 19th-century, while in the mid-seventies some six fish were sighted. Even now, after a massive clean-up programme by the Severn Trent Water Authority, few fish are known to make the spawning run. But the good news is that the Trent must be considered as one of Britain's most improved rivers.

Famous in the last few decades for its roach, the Trent now provides a tremendous variety of species for thousands of visiting anglers every year. With the purer water has come an explosion of bigger fish such as carp, chub and barbel. Bream, too, are thriving, adding another dimension to the section of the river that forces its way through the heart of Nottinghamshire's industry. Paradoxically it is the very industry which caused the Trent's downfall that now contributes to the quality of the Trent's angling. Heated power station and other industrial outlets not only encourage fish growth, but the warm water keeps fish moving throughout the year and there is enjoyable angling even in the depths of winter.

In the Nottingham area, the river undergoes a distinct change of character.

Upstream from the city the river is very fast-flowing over shallows and it is in the Long Eaton to Clifton stretches that some huge chub catches are taken. But once into the city the Trent has a more even and deeper flow in which high quality roach thrive. There is free fishing to be had along the 'Embankment' which runs upstream from Trent Bridge just a stone's throw from Nottingham Forest football stadium. From the railway bridge by the football ground down to Holme Pierrepoint, the Earl Manvers Angling Club controls the water, the boundary being at the yacht club. The angling club issues day tickets.

Moving downstream on the north bank, the next important angling area is from the Stoke Weir to the Gunthorpe road bridge (A6097). Roach and chub dominate the species caught here, with chub of up to 4lb being taken all year round. The section is controlled by the major angling association in the area, the Nottingham Federation, who sell day tickets on the bank. Included in the club's length is the once-famous 'Golden Mile' which produced many monster bags of roach that teemed in the water from an outfall upstream of this roadside reach. Parking is allowed on the road and the fishing is still good enough to attract plenty of visitors to the spot.

Float fishing with both stick and waggler floats brings results but some of the really big chub fall to anglers using ledger tackle, feeding the swim with bronze maggots. Much of the south bank in the area is controlled by Nottingham Angling Association and this, too, can be fished on a day ticket, although a 400-yard section above Gunthorpe Bridge is reserved for members only.

Below the Bridge, the chub population has really exploded and many major contests including the Trent Championship have been won with catches from this reach. Float fishing, holding a bait back against the flow achieves the best results from this stretch, where two meadows on the north side from Gunthorpe weir are controlled by the Nottingham Federation issuing day tickets. Two further meadows downstream are private, but from the Dover Beck through Caythorpe to Hoveringham, Midland Angling Association take charge and there follows a stretch to Causeway Dyke owned by Nottingham Angling Association. Both clubs issue day tickets.

Below the Dyke towards Hazleford, a field upstream from the Star and Garter public house is owned by the pub and you can buy a ticket with your 'lunch'. Below the pub are several short-day ticket lengths, split by private reaches and the wise angler will read all the bank-side notices to avoid bailiff trouble.

Just outside Newark the river flow is split by the Newark Dyke, a water along which Newark and District bailiffs sell day tickets. Summer anglers are advised to try fishing hemp and tares on this water for some really bumper roach catches.

On the main river from Farndon Ferry down to the Dyke is Northern Angling Association water and the Nottingham Piscatorial Society have a members-only stretch into Newark. A short reach of the old river is, however, fishable on day tickets which may be obtained from Newark District Council, Kelham Hall.

Wollaton Hall, Nottingham

This exciting length of the Trent ends at Winthorpe, a major lake and river fishery controlled by the Water Authority itself. Chub

Camping
Newark: Trax Campsite ►►
Mainly level 60-pitch site near Southwell Racecourse
Open May–mid-Sep, no bookings
Nottingham: Green Acres ►►
Tel: (0602) 864892
Gently sloping 8-pitch site
Open all year, must book
Surprise View Trailer Park ►►►►►
Tel: (0602) 204695
Flat 50-pitch site
Open Apr–Sep, no bookings

Golfing
Mapperley (Nottingham):
Tel: (0602) 265611
Hilly course but with easy walking, 9 holes, 5327yds, par 70, SSS67
Newark:
Tel: (063 684) 282
Parkland course, 18 holes, 6461yds, par 72, SSS71
Oxton (Nottingham):
Tel: (060 744) 3545
Testing heathland course, 18 holes, 6630yds, par 72, SSS72

Riding
Newark: Wellow Park Stables, Wellow
Tel: (0623) 851040
Nottingham: 'St Clements' Lodge Riding School, Woods Lane, Calverton
Tel: (060 744) 2524

Walking Trails
Gunthorpe Rural Walk: 4m (2½hr) signposted riverside walk. Start from Gunthorpe car park, near Unicorn Inn, Gunthorpe, Lowdham

General
Newark: Newark District Council Museum: local art & history
Open all year (ex Thu afternoons)
Tel: (0636) 702358
Newstead Abbey: rebuilt priory famed as Lord Byron's home, 8m N of Nottingham off A611
Open mid-Apr–Sep daily 2–6
Nottingham: Industrial Museum: local industrial history including hosiery, lace, printing
Open all year, times vary
Tel: (0602) 284602
Museum of Costume & Textiles: clothing, furnishings & tapestry c1750–1950
Open all year daily 10–5

are a major catch here and the swim feeder takes the best fish. But take a lot of bait – up to a gallon of maggots will be needed for a good day's fishing.

The Trent skirts an area beloved of little boys, Sherwood Forest, and although the acres of royal hunting woodlands have dwindled over the centuries, enough of the Forest and memories of Robin Hood survive to make an evergreen holiday haunt. There are three campsites in Nottingham alone.

Maid Marion is said to have lived at Blidworth and in the 15th-century hilltop church, Will Scarlet reputedly lies buried. The wicked Sheriff's stronghold, Nottingham, is a county, university and manufacturing town dominated by an imposing castle. Founded by William the Conqueror, it tops 133 feet of sheer rock. Inside is an art gallery, original dungeons and a museum, one of several in Nottingham. Of particular family interest is Brewhouse Yard museum where period rooms and thematic displays illustrate mediaeval life with working models which *can* be touched. The city's associations with hosiery, lace and tobacco are featured at the Industrial Museum which is located in the Courtyard Buildings of Wollaton Park.

Probably the best way to discover Nottingham is to follow one of its three walking trails – the Lace Market, Georgian and William Booth.

Newark, with its ruined castle, fine houses, ancient inns and wide market square, received its share of notable visitors, also. Close to an intersection of the Fosse Way and the (former) Great North Road it made a handy overnight stop for travellers such as Jeanie Deans, the heroine of Scott's Heart of Midlothian, who slept at the former Saracen's Head en route for London from Scotland. Gladstone made a speech here, Prince Rupert was a guest before the Civil War and Lord Byron was a frequent visitor. His ancestral home, Newstead Abbey, is only a few miles away and both the house, stuffed with mementoes, and the peaceful gardens are open in summer. Nearby is the ancient Pilgrims' Oak of Sherwood Forest.

Steeped in the history of Olde England, this part of Nottinghamshire has long been a happy hunting ground for campers and picnickers from the industrial Midlands, Yorkshire and Lancashire. Now that the waters of the Trent are enjoying a rejuvenation, this spot has added attractions for weekends or longer holiday visits, with plenty to do and see.

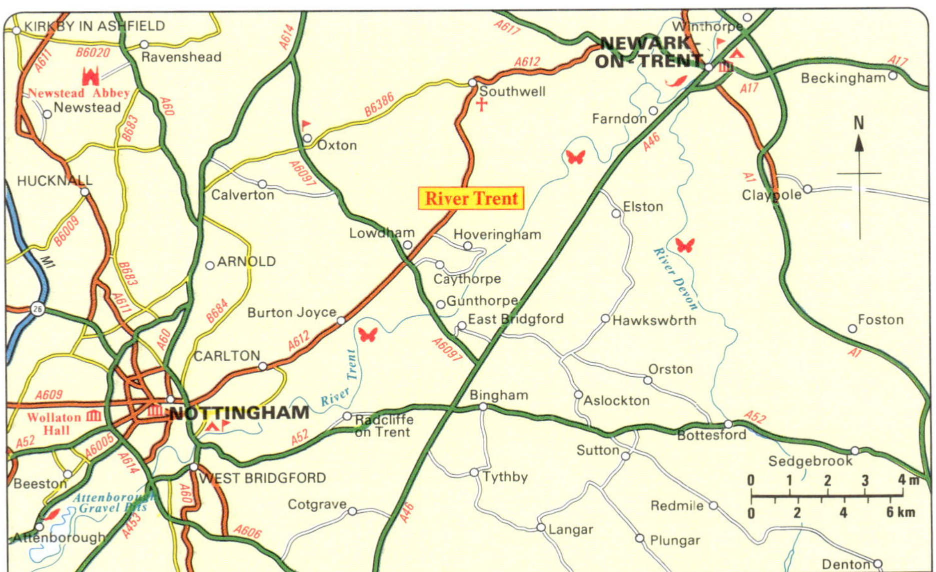

Attenborough Gravel Pits
Complex of 5 pits yields good bream, roach and tench – 3m SW of Nottingham
Daily tickets: Angler's Corner, Osmaston Road, Derby
Tel: (0332) 43870
Water Authority: as River Devon

River Devon
An improving stretch for coarse fishing
Free fishing from Springhouse Inn to Newark Dyke
Water Authority: STWA, Abelson House, Coventry Road, Sheldon, Birmingham
Tel: (021 743) 4222

Newark Dyke
Noted coarse fishery with quality roach
Daily tickets (on bank): between Farndon and Newark
Water Authority: as River Devon

Angler's Directory for the South East and East Midlands

Clubs and Associations

Abingdon & District Angling & Re-stocking Association (R Pitson), 11 Finmore Close, Abingdon, Oxfordshire
Tel: (0235) 25140

Broadstairs & St Peter's Sea Angling Society (H A Moor), 54 Stanley Road, Broadstairs, Kent
Tel: (0843) 69892

Colchester Angling Society (N Binks), 7 Churnwood Close, Colchester, Essex
Tel: (0206) 863649

Colnes Angling Society (J R Cowlin), 29 Burrows Road, Earls Colne, Colchester, Essex

Deal Angling Club (Ms H Green), c/o The Marina, Deal, Kent

Deal & Walmer Angling Association (R L Emmins), 29 The Strand, Walmer, Kent

Gt Yarmouth, Gorleston & District Angling Association (W Platten), 1 Audley Street, Gt Yarmouth, Norfolk
Tel: (0493) 4887

Hadleigh & District Angling Society (J Hill), 18 Highland Road, Hadleigh, Suffolk

Harwich & Dovercourt Angling Club (S A Delves), 32 Larksfield Crescent, Vine Gardens, Dovercourt, Essex
Tel: (025 55) 2760

Huntingdon Angling Society (W Wallis), 8 Clayton's Way, Huntingdon, Cambridgeshire
Tel: (0480) 58935

Isle of Wight Federation of Angling Clubs (R E Winship), Robreena, West Hill Road, Ryde
Tel: (0983) 64259

Lawford & Manningtree Angling Society (R W Nunn), Mistley Hall Cottage, Clacton Road, Mistley, Manningtree, Essex

London Anglers' Association (F Staples), 25 Nayland Road, Bures, Norfolk
Tel: (0787) 227555

Lymington & District Sea Fishing Club (K F Baveridge), 51 Gore Road, New Milton, Hampshire

Margate Fishing Club (HQ), Saracen's Head, High Street, Margate, Kent
Tel: (0843) 23578

Midland Angling Association (W Oldham), 57 Albury Drive, Aspley, Nottinghamshire

Newark & District Piscatorial Federation (J N Garland), 58 Riverside Road, Newark, Northamptonshire
Tel: (0636) 702962

Northampton Nene Angling Club (E M Love), 103 Charnwood Avenue, Weston Favell, Northampton
Tel: (0604) 409188

Norwich & District Angling Club (J C Braithwaite), 4 Cranage Road, Norwich, Norfolk
Tel: (0603) 25682

Nottingham Angling Association (S Simpson), 92 Main Street, Bulwell, Nottinghamshire

Old Centrals Angling Club, 130 Grosvenor Place, Margate, Kent

Oxford & District Anglers' Association (F Jones), 20 Merlin Road, Littlemore, Oxford
Tel: (0865) 770234

Royal Ramsgate Invicta Angling Club (B A Kirkaldie), 67 Boundary Road, Ramsgate, Kent
Tel: (0843) 584162

St Ives & District Fish Preservation & Angling Society (D Denton), 49 Little Farthing Close, St Ives, Cambridgeshire

St Neots & District Angling Society (S E Smith), 10 River Terrace, St Neots, Cambridgeshire
Tel: (0480) 75995

Sandwich & District Angling Society (M J Roe), 6 The Ridgeway, Cliftonville, Margate, Kent

Stamford-Welland Angling Club (K Bone), 126 Northumberland Avenue, Stamford, Lincolnshire
Tel: (0780) 4325

Sudbury & District Angling Association (B Roberts), 45 Chelsworth Avenue, Gt Cornard, Sudbury, Suffolk

Tackle Shops

Abingdon
Haines, Stert Street

Colchester
Home & Sports, 31a St Botolphs Street
Tel: (0206) 5382

Deal
The Angler, King Street
Tel: (030 45) 4573
Channel Angling, Deal Pier
Tel: (030 45) 3104
Dinkey's Den, Beach Street

Dovercourt
Sherwood Tackle, 6 The Kingsway
Tel: (025 55) 4602

East Cowes
Bruce's, 3 Clarence Road
Tel: (0983) 293291

Gt Yarmouth
Pownall & Sons Ltd, 74 Regent Road
Tel: (0493) 2873

Harwich
G K Cann, 4 Market Street
Tel: (025 55) 2959

Huntingdon
County Angling & Sports, High Street
Sports & Fashions, High Street
Tel: (0480) 54541

Lymington
Smith's Sports, 25 Queen Street
Tel: (0590) 73834

Margate
Kingfisheries, 34 King Street
Tel: (0843) 23866

Melton Mowbray
J F Green, 36 Nottingham Street
Tel: (0664) 4757

Newark
G M Purvis, 41 Castle Gate

Northampton
Gilders, 148 Wellingborough Road
Tel: (0604) 36723
Sportsman's Lodge, 44 Kingsthorpe Road, Kingsthorpe Hollow
Tel: (0604) 713399

Norwich
John's Tackle Den, 18 Bridewell Alley
Tel: (0603) 614114

Nottingham
Redmayne & Todd, Carrington Street
Tel: (0602) 51904
T Watson, 1 Oak Street
Tel: (0602) 609561

Oakham
Rutland Sports, 20 Catmore Street
Tel: (0572) 2675

Oxford
J Wilkins, 39a James Street
Tel: (0865) 43469

Potter Heigham
Latham Stores
Tel: (069 27) 388

Ramsgate
Anglers' Retreat, 32 Addington Street
Decca Sports, 4 Kent Place
Tel: (0843) 53128

Ryde
The Tackle Box, 73 High Street

St Ives
Handicrafts, Bridge Street

Sandwich
J P Francis, 13 The Butchery
Tel: (0304) 612237

Stamford
Sports & Hobbies, All Saints Street
Tel: (0780) 4524

Sudbury
The Swim & Pitch, Tower Lane
Tel: (0787) 74066

Walmer
Down's Tackle Shop, The Strand

Wellingborough
A Watts, 18 Cannon Street
Tel: (0933) 226718

Water Authorities

Anglian Water Authority, Diploma House, Grammar School Walk, Huntingdon, Cambridgeshire
Tel: (0480) 56181

Anglian Water Authority (Essex Rivers Division), 129 Springfield Road, Chelmsford, Essex
Tel: (0245) 64721

Anglian Water Authority (Rivers Division), Yare House, 62–64 Thorpe Road, Norwich, Norfolk
Tel: (0603) 615161

Severn Trent Water Authority, Abelson House, 2297 Coventry Road, Sheldon, Birmingham, West Midlands
Tel: (021 743) 4222

Severn Trent Water Authority (Lower Trent Division), Mapperley Hall, Lucknow Avenue, Nottingham
Tel: (0602) 608161

Southern Water Authority, Guildbourne House, Chatsworth Road, Worthing, Sussex
Tel: (0903) 205252

Thames Water Authority, 2nd Floor, Reading Bridge House, Reading, Berkshire
Tel: (0734) 593333

3
Wales &
West Midlands

Warwickshire Avon

Evesham – Stratford-upon-Avon

Water Authority
Severn Trent Water Authority – two types of rod licence issued. Salmon licence (Severn area only) covers for trout and freshwater fish – one day and season licences available. Severn and Trent areas trout and freshwater fish licence – annual and 28-day licences available. Licences sold by tackle shops. Information on River Avon from: STWA, Area Recreation Officer, 64 Albert Road North, Malvern, Hereford & Worcester
Tel: (6845) 61511

Angling Associations
Birmingham Angling Association
Hazeldine Angling Association
Stratford-upon-Avon Angling Society
Worcester and District United Angling Association

Tackle Shops
B Brookes, Bristol Road South, Birmingham
Austin Clisset, Pershore Road, Birmingham
Evesham Sports Centre, Bridge Street, Evesham
Joan Heritage, Merstow Green, Evesham
W H Lane, London Road, Coventry
Other ticket sources: Mr E Huxley, Hampton Ferry and Stratford-on-Avon Corporation bailiffs

Close Seasons
Salmon: September 30 – February 2, *trout:* September 30 – March 18, *coarse fish:* March 15 – June 15

Camping
Harvington: Carr's Caravans Ltd ►►►
Tel: (0386) 870446
Grassy site 4m N of Evesham (no tents)
Open mid-Mar–Oct, must book Jul–Aug
Honeybourne: Ranch Caravan Park ►►►
Tel: (0386) 830744
100-pitch farmland site (no tents)
Open Spring Bank holiday–Oct
Tiddington: Elms ►►
Tel: (0789) 292312
Level 50-pitch site 1m from Stratford
Open Apr–Oct, must book

Golfing
Evesham:
Tel: (0386) 860395
Scenic parkland course, 9 holes, 6228yds, par 71, SSS70
Stratford-upon-Avon:
Tel: (0789) 2669
Attractive parkland course, 18 holes, 6296yds, par 72, SSS70

General
Bidford-on-Avon: Domestic Fowl Trust: Unusual collection of ducks, hens, geese & turkeys, set in 4-acre park off the B4085
Open Apr–Oct daily 10.30–6 (ex Mon)
Tel: (078 988) 2442
Evesham: The Almonry: 14th-century half-timbered building, housing local history museum
Open Apr–Sep afternoons (ex Mon & Wed)
Tel: (0386) 6944
Shottery: Anne Hathaway's Cottage: thatched Elizabethan home where Shakespeare's wife was born
Open all year times vary
Tel: (0789) 292100
Stratford-upon-Avon: Louis Tussaud's: waxworks full of famous names
Open all year
Tel: (0789) 5880
Model Car Museum: international collection of over 19 000 miniature vehicles
Open all year 9–5.30
Tel: (0789) 2233
Shakespeare's Birthplace: the half-timbered dwelling where the world-famous dramatist was born
Open all year times vary
Tel: (0789) 292325

Warwickshire's River Avon, one of the most important tributaries of the Severn system, is steeped in history as it meanders from under the shadow of Warwick Castle, through the heart of Shakespeare country to the ancient abbeys of Evesham, Pershore and Tewkesbury. In more recent times the Avon has made a name for itself as one of the main angling playgrounds for the fishermen of the big industrial cities such as Birmingham and Coventry. Famed as a match river, the Avon has been the training ground for Britain's top rods – men like Birmingham Angling Association skipper Clive Smith and the international anglers Ken Giles and Mark Downes.

This is, however, a river that has suffered considerable damage to fish stocks and habitats from industrial pollution. The worst affected stretches are considered to be those centred around Warwick, in the Avon's upper waters. All the signs are that the Avon is now making a remarkable recovery and is even now among the best roach and chub rivers in Britain. Some measure of the sport available can be drawn from the Avon's current match record, a fine bag of 75lb taken near Eckington.

While it is chub that makes up the really big weights of match catches, the bream population is increasing and the species is establishing itself in ever more swims in this water. Roach, dace and perch are all here in reasonable numbers and some respectable carp are now being taken in waters around and below Evesham. The middle reaches, centring on this market-gardening town, provide some of the best pike fishing in the autumn.

Facilities for visiting fishermen are very good considering that long sections are controlled by large Midlands associations like the Birmingham Angling Association. In fact, you would be well-advised to join up for a season with this club if you are spending a week or more in the area – a season ticket gives you access to almost half the river.

It is this association that has much of the fishing immediately above the tourist haven of Stratford-upon-Avon, a stretch extending into the town's Avon Meadows area. The local authority also runs a day ticket stretch below the lido and into the town centre – local tackle shops sell these tickets.

Throughout this reach of the river the average depth is around five feet and the water has a nice pace that responds well to stick float methods which run the bait slightly slower than the current. Maggots, casters and hempseed will all take fish on the right day but do not waste groundbait on the Avon here – these fish are renowned for their discrimination and cunning.

A workable method is to set a float slightly overdepth, tied top and bottom, and work the bait through an area fed by regular small handfuls of hook-bait. This should bring out the cleverest roach, dace and chub.

Below Stratford, Birmingham Angling Association controls one bank while the other is administered by Hazeldine Angling Association. There is a two-mile section of the right bank at Luddington that is available only to members of the Stratford-upon-Avon Angling Society. Downstream to Welford there is not a lot of chance for visitors as clubs control the water, however, the Four Alls Inn owns a fishery close to the bridge on the A439. Around Bidford, Birmingham Angling Association have one bank and the Worcester and District United Angling Association (a club that issues honorary membership cards) have the other bank.

One of the few free fishing stretches is to be found at Cleeve, where the Severn Trent Water Authority opens the banks to all-comers with a rod licence. This is a very pleasant reach of the river which holds some very big chub, dace and roach. The stick float with maggot or casters is one of the foremost methods here, too. Other good day ticket waters are on offer at Court Farm, Offenham (left bank and the weir) and the Bridge Inn (a short stretch on the opposite bank).

In Evesham itself the waters are superb and it is, as a result, the venue for several major events in the angling calendar. Depths here vary from six to fifteen feet and some accurate long-range casting is required to get the best from many of the pegs.

At Hampton Ferry, day tickets can be bought at the ferry cottage and bailiffs patrol the banks selling tickets for the Town Meadows. Do make sure that the water you would like to fish is not booked for a match during your stay here. As a general rule this, and other stretches of the Avon, will give the best results if you use float tackle on fine lines and with small hooks. Bait swims with loose feed but, nevertheless, some good chub are taken in fast water by swimfeeders.

In this whole area it is very difficult to get away from the life and legend of William Shakespeare. Stratford itself is a shrine to the playwright bard and is the first stop for many Americans doing a round-Britain coach tour. Here you can see the house in which the dramatist was born, containing relics and documents of his life, visit the Memorial Theatre for a play or to view the Gallery Exhibition of costumes. Note that if you do want to see action on the stage booking in advance is advisable. Stratford also has rowing boats for hire on the river and the bizarre pleasures of Louis Tussaud's Waxworks and Model Car Museum.

The former Roman camp of Alcester is north of the river and nearby is Ragley Hall, home of the historic Seymour family. While there is a wealth of English and French paintings, furniture and porcelain in the house, it is the grounds that will attract most families. The gardens include lakeside picnicking spots, a nature trail and a woodland adventure playground. Tickets are available at the gate for fishing the lake. Lovers of gardens should head for Pleck Gardens nearer the town. Three acres of grounds around three large ponds brim with roses, heather, azaleas and rhododendrons – there is also a large collection of budgerigars!

South of Evesham, walkers are in the Cotswolds where a maze of small footpaths and the well-signposted Cotswold Way take you over rolling hills to small unspoiled villages of soft yellow stone. To the west of the town is the Delamere Bird Garden offering to tourists the unlikely combination of a large bird collection, a zoo of pet animals and model railway layouts. Undoubtedly Evesham's finest time is in late spring, when the small market gardens of the Vale are in full bloom.

During May, the town holds a regatta on the river but the Avon is always bustling with small craft and there are some beautiful riverside walks in the area.

The countryside of the Avon, its fishing and many other visitors' delights are very much at England's heart with easy access from both the M5 and the M1/M45. Some intimate and friendly campsites, a good sprinkling of self-catering holiday homes and lots of opportunities to enjoy the great outdoors make the area a wise choice for a short family break.

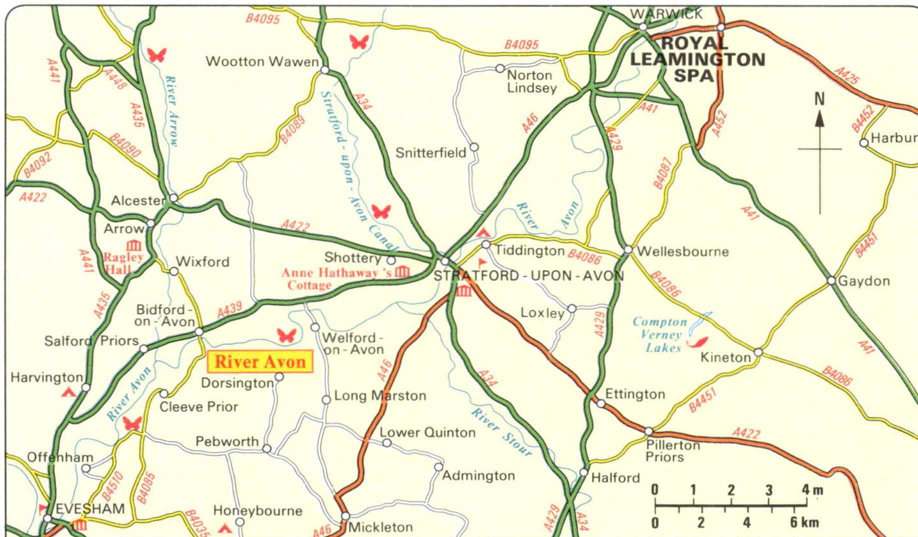

River Arrow
From its source north of Redditch flows to join the Avon at Salford Priors – mostly coarse fishing with some chance of trout
Daily tickets: Fish Hotel, Wixford
Tel: (078 988) 2478
Water Authority: STWA (Severn River Division)
Tel: (068 45) 61511

Compton Verney Lakes
Good coarse fishery 8m SE of Stratford
Daily tickets: Mr Shoeman, Kineton Garage, Kineton
Tel: (0926) 640570 (for North Lake) or Park Farm, Kineton
Tel: (0926) 640258 (for South Lake)
Water Authority: as River Arrow

Stratford-upon-Avon Canal
Occasional catches of bream, gudgeon, roach and perch, especially around Wootton Wawen
For alternative payment system contact: Birmingham Angling Association
Water Authority: as River Arrow

Fishing on a weir near Offenham

River Wye

Symonds Yat – Hereford

Water Authority
Welsh National Water Development Authority – rod licence system is complex. For the River Wye a coarse fishing licence can be obtained on a season or day basis. For salmon fishing below Llanwrthwl Bridge a Class A licence is required, above this point a Class C licence is required. Contact WNDWA, Cambrian Way, Brecon, Powys
Tel: (0874) 3181

Angling Associations
Birmingham Angling Association
Hereford and District Angling Association
Ross-on-Wye Angling Club
Worcester and District United Angling Association

Tackle shops
Allsports, Barton Street, Gloucester
A Brookes, Bristol Road South, Birmingham
H Hatton, Owen Street, Hereford
Stan Lewis, Severn Side South, Worcester
F Perkins, Commercial Road, Hereford

Close Seasons
Salmon: October 26 – January 25 in Class C waters – October 1 – January 25 for Class A
Coarse fishing: March 15 – June 15 (Note special rules on use of maggots.)

The Wye is unquestionably one of Britain's loveliest rivers. Rising on Plynlimon, a boggy mass of a mountain in mid-Wales which also feeds the infant Severn, it rejoins this river below Chepstow. In its path it takes a series of ever larger loops across much of the southern border country between England and Wales, forming the border itself for the last twenty miles or so of its course. It flows beneath strategic border castles and past the remains of the once-regal Tintern Abbey, through the picturesque gorge of Symonds Yat and the towns of Hereford and Ross-on-Wye. The Wye is a sightseers' river, a canoeists' river – but most of all it is an anglers' river. It is one of the best game waters in Britain and is correspondingly difficult and expensive to fish. Anglers lucky enough to spend time here will, however, have the chance to equal the local record of a 59½lb salmon, or to more modestly try their skills in the relatively fast waters for dace over 1lb, roach of nearly 3lb, chub around the 6½lb mark and even the occasional bream over 7½lb.

The upper reaches of the river are a rough and tumble of fast water over rocky beds, with the banks very much the preserve of the rod syndicates. Coarse fishing becomes more prominent in the waters from Hereford to Builth Wells but here we concentrate on the many meanders of the Wye from the Hereford area down to Symonds Yat and the wild Forest of Dean with its many opportunities for angling, camping and walking.

Since the various fishing managements of the Wye are principally interested in the preservation of game fishing, you should note that on many waters there is a ban on the use of maggots from March 14–October 26, and in some areas a complete ban on coarse fishing until this end of the salmon season. Once again it is worth investigating the taking out of membership of the Birmingham Angling Association, a large controller of rights, or honorary membership of the Worcester and District United Angling Association, although there are many reaches that can be fished on day tickets from tackle shops or inns.

Be prepared on the tackle front, too. The Wye is no place for fine tackle and small hooks. Big balsa floats fastened top and bottom and three or four AAA shot some eighteen inches above the hook will sink the bait down to the fish feeding levels. Cast with an underarm swing and then try to ease the tackle through in a straight line with the flow. Bites tend to be savage and a tight line to the float will ensure few fish are missed.

Fishing on any section of the Wye calls for a lot of bait. On the stretches where maggots are allowed (and at the times they are allowed) you can get through a gallon in a five-hour session! The trick is to keep feeding steadily all the time. If you feed too much at a time the fish drop further downstream from the swim. If you are using bread, fishing with large lumps of flake should lure one or two very big chub – but again, take a couple of large fresh loaves with you to ensure a good catch.

In Hereford itself there is day ticket fishing on six and a half miles of water controlled by the Hereford and District Club. The water starts at Belmont, goes through Castle Park and downstream to around the railway at Bartonsham. These are chub, roach and dace reaches, with many fine fish taken every year. The club also has day ticket waters at Holme Lacy and Fownhope. Also at Holme Lacy is a section controlled by the Hereford tackle firm of H Hatton.

Between Holme Lacy and Ross-on-Wye

Wading in the Wye

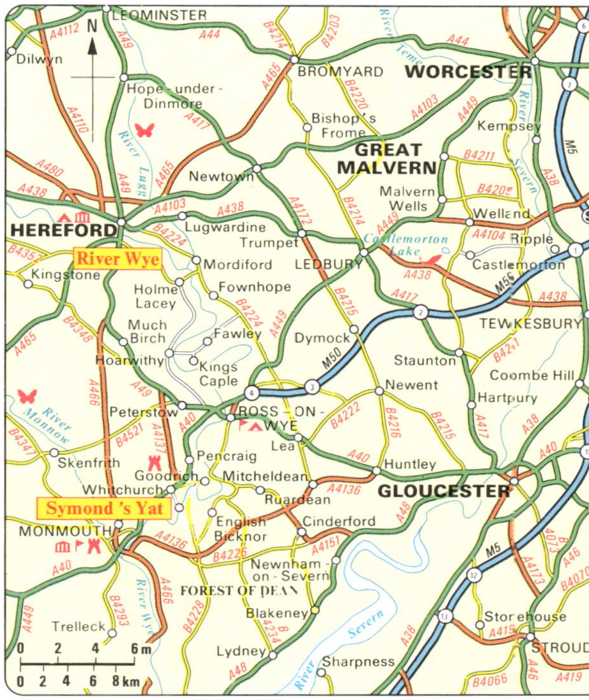

Castlemorton Lake
Free coarse fishing, near Ledbury
Water Authority: STWA, Abelson House, 2297 Coventry Road, Sheldon, Birmingham
Tel: (021 743) 4222

River Lugg
Major Wye tributary with excellent trout and coarse fish, but ticket chances limited
Daily tickets: Longworth Hall Hotel, Lugwardine, Hereford (residents only) or B Thorpe and Partners, Fishery Dept, Broad Street, Hereford
Tel: (0432) 6202
Water Authority: WNWDA (Wye River Division), Cambrian Way, Brecon, Powys
Tel: (0874) 3181

River Monnow
Prolific trout waters, but ticket opportunities not good
Daily tickets: Priory Motel, Skenfrith or Monmouth & District Angling Society (F Hughes), Brook Cottage, Monmouth, Gwent
Tel: (0600) 3793
Water Authority: WNWDA (Wye River Division), Cambrian Way, Brecon, Powys

there is good access to the river from the network of small lanes lacing the area. There are fishable stretches at Hoarwithy, Kings Caple and near Fawley.

Ross is an old market town perched high on a bluff over the river. Birmingham Angling Association has a half-mile water for members close to the town, but from the rowing club down to Wilton Bridge the Ross Angling Club controls a prolific coarse fishing stretch.

South of Ross, some smaller riparian owners take over and it is always worthwhile approaching farmers, inns and hotels for a day's fishing. Above the hotel at Symond's Yat, the Birmingham Angling Association takes control again and Worcester and District have rights on the Old Forge length. In this most picturesque part of the Wye's plain stage, chub and dace dominate the fish population and bread baits are the favourite local lure.

Surrounding this famous gorge with its twin guardian rocks – the Yat Rock itself dominating the scene and facing the Coldwell rocks on the Gloucestershire bank – is the Forest of Dean. Much of the woods are unchanged since the days when wood was hauled from here to Severnside shipyards and coal was dug by hand to fire the industrial revolution.

The Forest, large parts of it still a variety of deciduous trees, is Forestry Commission land and there have been major efforts to attract campers here. Bracelands and Christchurch are two of the big sites in the area, but there are also several smaller camps, some of them with only a water pipe for the self-reliant camper.

The Forest is laced with nature trails, walks and orienteering courses. Around Symonds Yat and Christchurch are a number of way-marked walks suitable for families to enjoy the views across the river.

The country between the Yat and Hereford is lush pastureland dotted with occasional cider orchards. Just a few of the local farms still make this potent brew by traditional methods and they are well worth tracking down. Ross-on-Wye is one regional centre that must be visited especially on cattle market day (Friday) when streets and pubs throng with more locals than visitors. Half-timbered houses, an old butter-market and a maze of small shops selling local produce and antiques are delightful to spend an hour browsing around.

Hereford has similar attractions – but with the advantage of a large covered market. Close to the town centre is the Bulmers Railway Centre (sponsored by the cider company), a collection of engines and rolling stock sited at the former Midlands Railway goods yard. Actor David Garrick was born at the Raven Inn and there are some who believe that the infamous Nell Gwynne launched her sales career here, too. But Hereford's history is more sober – it has been the seat of a bishop since 672 AD and the now largely Norman cathedral is famous for its rare books and documents including the 14th-century Mappa Mundi.

The Wye wends through a land of many castles. Perhaps the most interesting is Goodrich, built from the 12th–14th-century as a moated defence point from which to repel and subjugate Welsh marauders. The Talbots, Earls of Shrewsbury lived here until Cromwellian troops breached the walls with a mortar known as Roaring Meg, now found on Castle Green.

It is the very rural nature of the industries along the Wye's banks that has preserved this attractive water from the worst effects of modern pollution dangers. This has made it a river which can still be enjoyed to the fullest by all users of water and one that yields regular large catches of superb fish.

Camping
Hereford: Trax Campsite ►►
Quiet 60-pitch site
Open Jun–Sep, no bookings
Ross-on-Wye: Cottage Caravan Park ►►►
Tel: (0989) 2362
Partly sloping 50-pitch meadowland site
Open Mar–Oct, must book Jul–Aug

Golfing
Monmouth:
Tel: (0600) 2212
Scenic downland course 1m E of town centre, 9 holes, 5600yds, par 68, SSS66
Ross-on-Wye:
Tel: (098 982) 267
Undulating course with well-screened fairways, 18 holes, 6491yds, par 72, SSS72

General
Goodrich: Goodrich Castle: 12th–14th-century fortress
Open all year
Hereford: Bulmers Railway Centre: interesting locomotives & static displays for steam buffs
Open Apr–Sep steam weekends one Sun per month
Tel: (0432) 4791
Hereford Museum & Art Gallery: Roman remains, local geology, natural history, etc
Open all year (ex Sun) 10–6
Tel: (0432) 68121 ext 207
Monmouth:
Monmouth Castle: 12th-century fortress, birthplace of Henry V
Open all year
Monmouth Museum: local history plus relics & mementoes of Nelson
Open all year (Sun – afternoons only)
Mordiford: Sutton Court: late 18th-century mansion with notable fireplaces & doors
Open May–Sep (Sun only)
Tel: (043 273) 268

River Severn

Shrewsbury – Newtown

Water Authority
Severn Trent Water Authority – two types of rod licence issued. Salmon licence (Severn area only) covers for trout and freshwater fish – day and season licences available. Severn and Trent area trout and freshwater fish licence – annual and 28-day licences available. Licences sold by tackle shops. Information on River Severn from: STWA, Area Recreation Officer, 64 Albert Road North, Malvern, Hereford & Worcester
Tel: (06845) 61511

Angling Associations
Birmingham Angling Association
Crewe Pioneers
Cheshire Angling Association
Warrington Angling Association

Tackle Shops (and Licence Agents)
H Bebb, Short Bridge Street, Newtown
A Bond, Hall Street, Welshpool
Ebrall Bros, Smithfield Road, Shrewsbury
Mrs L McCrae, Roverband Caravan Park, Llangadfan

Close Seasons
Salmon: September 30 – February 2, *trout:* September 30 – March 18, *coarse fish:* March 15 – June 15

At just over 200 miles, the Severn is England's longest river. Rising in the Plynlimon area, close to the source of the Wye, the Severn describes a large arc across Wales and the borders before descending across the rich fruit-growing areas of Hereford and Worcester and Gloucestershire to the vast estuary of the Bristol Channel.

The river holds almost every species of coarse fish, good stocks of brown trout in some areas and it has a very healthy run of salmon. It is a river that has become renowned for its barbel, a fish that has exploded in both number and sizes recorded. Today's barbel are almost certainly a result of energetic stocking by the angling newspaper *Angling Times* and the former river authority in the mid Fifties. While this was a policy pursued in the middle reaches of the river around Bridgnorth, good sized fish have certainly found their way up to and past Shrewsbury. This is a part of the Severn often ignored and frequently eclipsed by the big catches in the wider waters to the south. But if your weekend or holiday visit to the border falls close to the Severn do not miss out on the opportunity to try the hundreds of angling spots in this upper river which offer sport that still rates among the very best in Britain.

Close to the centre of the historic border town of Shrewsbury is the ideal sunny day spot for the family. While anglers in Quarry Park may occasionally share the waters with oarsmen from the Shrewsbury School boathouse, the river here is wide and there is very little intrusion. Both pleasure and match anglers take large chub in this length and they are well-known for putting up a hard fight. Angling children and fine tackle experts can find as much fun taking roach and dace. The water's pace is very steady and even the unluckiest visitor should get into fish by drifting a float only a rod length or so from the bank. Wasp grub, maggots, casters and hemp and tares in summer will all pull in good bags. These Shrewsbury town waters are available on day tickets sold by tackle shops. Visitors can also obtain Ditherington Angling Club tickets for nearby waters at Underdale, Sundorne and Belvedere (coarse and salmon tickets available but only for one week).

At Montford Bridge, which carries the Wales-bound A5 trunk road across the Severn, the river retains its width although it is noticeable that the barbel begin to fade out at this point and they are rarely seen in numbers. Pike are a prominent catch below the bridge, especially when the river is slightly coloured by rains in the higher reaches. Be prepared to move around a bit using a spinning rod and lures. Roach, chub and dace are also present in this water in considerable numbers.

Near Crew Green, the River Vyrnwy joins the Severn after its tumble down from the mountains surrounding its reservoir source. This major tributary has very good day ticket fishing on its banks but on the Severn, a mile below the confluence, fishing is free to Severn rod licence holders with access through the village of Melverley. This is a constantly changing section of the river, not only because of the Vyrnwy's influence but also due to the cold feeds into the Severn from the brooding Clywedog Reservoir.

However, above Vyrnwy there is some very good fishing for large chub and fish of around 5lb are taken regularly. Bread flake bait fished down the steadier runs is the technique that tends to take the bigger fish. Once again, membership of the Birmingham Angling Association will allow you to sample the waters at Crew Green itself and the lower Alberbury stretch.

The same club holds some water at Llandrinio just over the Welsh border. The club's rights in Wales also extend to the Pool Quay area, where roach enthusiasts have a sporting chance of landing specimen fish.

Here the river bends southward towards Welshpool and some considerable lengths come under the control of the Montgomeryshire Angling Association. Welshpool and Newtown tackle shops will give details of these waters, most of which can be fished on day tickets. Welshpool waters offer good chub and, if you would like a change, try for dace which run to 12oz or so. Pike are fished in this water but they are small and rarely make double figures. The river has markedly reduced in width and it is easily fished with float tackle and a 12–13-foot rod.

From Welshpool, the Severn begins to take on the character of a game river and although there are some high quality grayling and many coarse species to be taken, opportunities are somewhat limited by trout and salmon interests. Among the best stretches is the STWA fishery at Cilcewydd Bridge on the A490 just south of Welshpool. This again is a water with some free fishing for rod licence holders. Other free facilities in the area offered by the STWA are half a mile of the river in Newtown, and the short Llandinam coarse fishery near Caersws. An extension of this water from the confluence of the Trannon to a point some three miles upstream is an STWA game fishery available to visitors who hold the appropriate licence (day and season tickets from Mr Evans Jones, Broneirion Cottages, Llandinam).

The Severn is within striking distance of the wild Berwyn mountains and a favourite spot for walkers is Llanrhaeadr-ym-Mochnant. From the village, on the B4580, a narrow lane climbs a valley to reveal, at its head, one of the so-called seven wonders of Wales – the 240ft Pistyll Rhaeadr falls. For those who enjoy scenery, a visit to the falls could be combined with a trip to Lake Vyrnwy, a four-mile long reservoir supplying water to the Midlands.

Shrewsbury was, from very early times regarded as a splendid natural fortress, a habitation on a bluff over the Severn, looped about by the river and conveniently approachable only from the north. This martial aspect of what is today a picturesque old town of half-timber houses is reflected in the fact that there are no fewer than six regimental museums. It is

Castle Gates House, Shrewsbury – now privately owned, but the ornate sixteenth century facade still pulls the crowds on the way to the castle

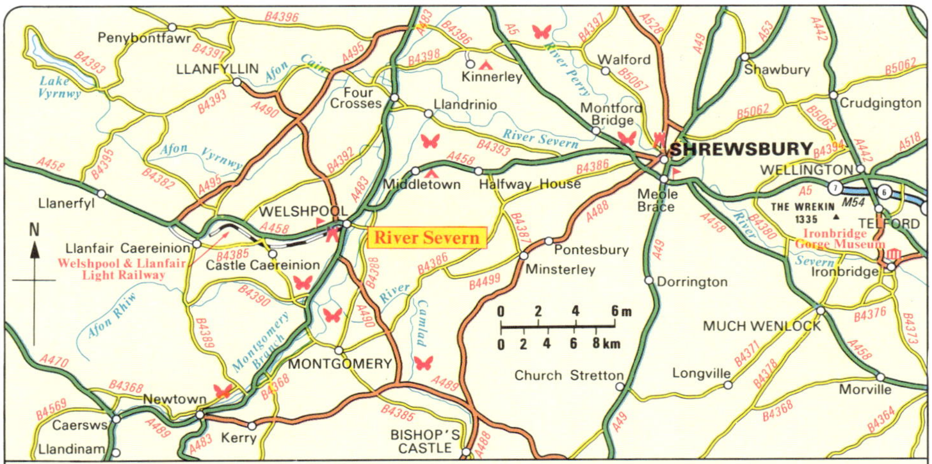

River Camlad
Small Severn tributary offering mixed fishing, south of Welshpool
Daily tickets: Millington's Tackle, Welshpool
Water Authority: STWA, Abelson House, 2297 Coventry Road, Sheldon, Birmingham
Tel: (021 743) 4222

Montgomery Branch
Scenic stretch of Shropshire Union Canal, largely overgrown but good fishing near Welshpool
Daily tickets (very limited): Cammell Laird Sports Club (Angling Section), 20 Clarendon Close, Cloughton, Birkenhead, Merseyside
Water Authority: as River Camlad

River Perry
Good for chub and dace, with some chance of roach
Daily tickets: Ebrall Bros, Shrewsbury
Tel: (0743) 3048
Water Authority: as River Camlad

also a town with two names both of which date from the 8th-century, when Offa took the town. Salop is derived from Sloppesbury, and Shrewsbury (now the preferred name) is a rendition of Scrobesbyrig.

Perhaps the most absorbing day out in the whole area is the Ironbridge Gorge Museum, a complex of industrial archaeological sites and displays centred around the 200-year-old iron bridge over the Severn. Within this small area, which played a key part in the Industrial Revolution, are displays of the manufacture of Coalport china, iron-founding, a natural bitumen well and other early industrial machinery.

Ironbridge serves as a reminder that the Severn was not only prized for its fishing. It was a major transport artery spreading the area's products over much of the west of England. In addition, canals such as the Shropshire Union carry produce across the Midlands.

Camping
Kinnerley: Cranberry Moss Camping & Caravan Park ►►►
Tel: (074 381) 441
Partly sloping 60-pitch site, 12m NW of Shrewsbury off A5
Open Apr–Sep, must book Jul–Aug
Middletown: Bank Farm Caravan Park ►►
Tel: (093 874) 260
Partly sloping 20-pitch site
Open Apr–Oct, must book public holidays

Golfing
Llanymynech (Oswestry):
Tel: (0691) 830542
Scenic downland course, 18 holes, 6107yds, par 70, SSS69
Shrewsbury:
Tel: (074 372) 2976
Parkland course, 18 holes, 6277yds, par 72, SSS70
Welshpool:
Tel: (068 686) 670
Rolling heathland course, 18 holes, 6070yds, par 71, SSS70

Walking Trails
Corbet Wood Nature Trail: 1m (¾hr) circular walk incorporating clifftop picnic area. Start from ½m along Clive Road, Preston Brockhurst on A49 9m N of Shrewsbury
Earl's Hill Trail: 1m (1hr) tough hill climb. Start from near Pontesbury on A488 6m SW of Shrewsbury
Merrington Green: 1¼m (1hr) commonland walk. Turn right at Walford Heath 6m N of Shrewsbury off B5067

General
Llanfair Caereinion: Welshpool & Llanfair Light Railway: 5½m steam railway track
Open Easter–Oct (Sat & Sun) plus daily Jun–Aug
Tel: (093 882) 441
Shrewsbury: Bear Steps: newly restored 14th-century cottage
Open all year (ex Sun) 10–5
Tel: (0743) 52019
Longden Coleham Pumping Station: two restored 1900 beam engines
Open all year (Wed–Fri) 2–5 for other times
Tel: (0743) 54811
Shrewsbury Castle: historic, partly 12th-century fortress
Open Easter–Oct 10–5 (ex Sun)
Tel: (0743) 52019
Welshpool: Powis Castle: mediaeval stronghold with fine tapestries
Open May–Sep (ex Mon & Tue) 2–6
Tel: (0938) 2554

Bala Lake and River Dee

Source – Llangollen

Water Authority
Welsh National Water Development Authority
A complex system of salmon/sea trout licences is operated. Waters of the Dee can be fished with a C category licence, tributaries with a D category licence (a C licence also covers D areas and all other fish) and licences are obtainable for season, week and day periods. A non-migratory trout licence (also covering coarse fish) covers the whole WNWDA area and is available for season week and day. A coarse fishing licence for the whole WNWDA area is available for a season or a day. Licences are widely available in the area:
Dee & Clwyd River Division
Tel: (0244) 45004
Brecon Head Office
Tel: (0874) 3181

Angling Associations
Bala and District Angling Association
Liverpool and District Angling Association
Llangollen Angling Association
Llanuwchllyn Angling Club
Midland Fly Fishers

Tackle dealers and other ticket sources
W N and H N Elbourn, 12 Chapel Street, Llangollen, Clwyd
R E Evans, Bradford House, Bala, Gwynedd
Golden Pheasant Hotel, Llynmawr, Dolywern, Wrexham, Clwyd
Gwynedd County Council, Lake Warden, 24 Fford Pensarn, Bala, Gwynedd
W A Jones, Berwyn Arms Hotel, Glyndyfrdwy, Corwen, Clwyd
W E Pugh, 74 High Street, Bala, Gwynedd
WNWDA, 2 Vicar's Lane, Chester, Cheshire

Close Seasons
Salmon: October 15 – March 1,
sea trout: September 30 – March 1,
trout: September 30 – March 1 (Bala Lake: August 14 – January 15; Llyn Celyn: October 1 – March 30)
Coarse fish: March 14 – June 16

Bala Lake is the largest natural sheet of water in Wales and local superstition has it that the headwaters of the Dee, rising on the slopes of Aran Mawddy in Gwynedd, flow through the lake without mixing with the gloomy waters. Whatever the truth of this rumour, Bala (or Llyn Tegid) does pose one mystery and that is the curious whitefish, the gwyniad.

Herring-like in appearance, this salmonid has a pattern of distribution which is accounted for only by the possibility that the genus has survived by being selectively landlocked after the last Ice Age. The gwyniad, locally prized as a good eating fish, has cousins in the Lake District, the schelly or skelly and in Loch Lomond, the powan. A one-pound fish is a good one and they are rarely caught on rod and line due to the depths at which they live and the tiny aquatic creatures on which they feed. The name 'gwyniad' is the Welsh for 'shining', an apt description in view of the many small, silver scales of this fish.

The gwyniad is far from the only angling attraction of Bala and the Dee. The lake teems with perch, roach and brown trout and puts up the occasional pike of 20lb or so. The Dee is a famous salmon river, running in a deep-cut valley, parallel with the A5 for many miles, before spilling on to the Cheshire plain and out to sea at Shofton. Here, only the upper waters from Llangollen, a regular home to those peculiarly Welsh festivals of verse and song, the Eisteddfods, are considered. This thirty miles of the Dee system is one of great contrasts, from the pricey salmon waters of Llangollen itself to the calm (and cheaper) depth of Bala. This stretch of the system is able to provide sport for all types of anglers, as well as having the backdrop of some of the most beautiful country in inland Wales.

The Dee starts life as the Little Dee and is joined by the modest streams of the Lliw and Twrch just before entering the lake. This is water of the Llanuwchllyn Angling Club and fly, worm and spinning are allowed to lure the small trout in these bubbling, rocky streams promising hours of absorbing sport.

Fishing Llyn Tegid is the preserve of Gwynedd County Council, with tickets available from several local sources and boats for hire from the town of Bala. Occasional trout of 3lb are pulled from the lake, although the average is closer to 10oz. A quirk of the water is that the trout come to maturity earlier than those in the river and from the opening of the season on January 15th they begin to provide excellent sport. The lake also fishes well for coarse fish and pike, perch, roach and eel are all present in good numbers.

For a change, drive six miles or so up the A4212 to the Llyn Celyn reservoir, a WNWDA trout fishery that is now coming to prominence in the area. This 800-acre manmade lake in the valley of the River Tryweryn is stocked with 10–12in fish annually and while both spinning and worm fishing are allowed, there is a section of the water reserved for fly fishing only. The local tip is to use Mallard and Claret, Black Pennel, or Snipe and Purple flies on size fourteen hooks to get up to your bag limit of six fish.

Local rods in the guise of the Bala and District Angling Association control a 600-yard day-ticketed stretch of the Dee near to the outlet from the lake and the whole of the River Hirnant running in a deep gorge accessible by the B4391. This narrow road rises over a steep mountain pass before tumbling again through a wooded hillside to Lake Vyrnwy.

Fishing and sailing on Bala Lake

The course of the Dee follows the B4401 back-road to Corwen from Bala, a road on which there are several campsites. Sad to relate, the fishing is controlled by private interests, although if you are a regular visitor to the area it is worth joining the Corwen Angling Association who have several beats in the area.

The next opportunity for ticket fishing is on the Glyndyfrdwy Preserves Water, a one and three-quarter-mile beat of the Dee on the right bank from Tyn Celyn to the Glyndyfrdwy Bridge. This is a fly fishing-only stretch and separate tickets are available for salmon/sea trout and trout/grayling. Average weights in this stretch are 10oz for trout and 9oz for grayling.

The Dee is a fine salmon river ranking only below the Wye and the Usk in Wales for the quality and quantity of fish. Much of the sport develops in our chosen stretch in the later months of the spring sun, peaking in June–August. Salmon interests have a strong grip on the Llangollen area and rods are to a certain extent limited. It pays to follow up every opportunity, however – who knows when the last ticket available will turn up trumps with an enormous catch?

Midland Fly Fishers control four miles of the right bank below the Glyndyfrdwy reach, with day tickets available, like those of the Preserve Water, from the Berwyn Arms Hotel in the village. Llangollen Angling Association is the next in line with a number of beats totalling six miles in the area from Llantysilio into the town itself – full details are available from ticket agent W N and H N Elbourn in Llangollen. Local regulations forbid natural baits before May 1st and it is fly fishing-only on waters above the Chain Bridge. A limited number of Liverpool and District Angling Association salmon tickets are available on a left bank stretch near the Chain Bridge.

If you are lucky enough to stay at the Ponsonby or Hand Hotels, guests can buy tickets, to the left and right hand banks respectively, for short beats below the Llangollen Road Bridge. Another hotel worth trying for day ticket stretches is the Golden Pheasant, Llwynmawr, Dolywern, Wrexham which has rights on the Alwen, Dee and Ceiriog.

Most visitors to the area will choose to stay around Corwen and Bala, where there are a considerable number of small guesthouses, farmhouse holidays and campsites. It is to Bala that many families will gravitate for amusement, too. It is a stimulating walking area and there are several stables in the Dee valley where ponies can be hired by the day or hour for a leisurely exploration of the nearby woods, lakes and hills.

Bala, locked in the hills, has never had ideal weather and sailing enthusiasts value the broad expanse of the lake for the liveliness of the water and the rapid changes in conditions. The Bala Sailing Club welcomes visitors.

Children love steam engines and even if you cannot get up steam to trek across the mountains to the Festiniog or Tal-y-llyn Railways, Bala has its own. A short length of line and a rolling stock exhibition are to be seen between Llangower and Llanuwchllyn on the lake's south east shore.

Llangollen was once an important town on the Shropshire Union Canal. A museum of canal exhibits and rides by a horse-drawn barge to Pentrefelis, a mile away, commemorates the fact. Earlier Welsh history is to be found at Eiseg's Pillar, a rock said to have been erected to the memory of a chieftain who annexed Powys from the English in the 8th-century. Take the road from here to World's End where, far from experiencing Armageddon, you can take a nature trail round a limestone gorge and have panoramic views of the Dee valley.

This is very much an area for the self-sufficient family – and of course there is none so self-sufficient as a family that can dine off a meal of fresh Dee trout.

Camping
Bala: Penybont Touring Park ►►
Tel: (0678) 520549
Part-sloping 75-pitch site (25 caravans)
Open Apr–Sep, must book Jul–Aug
Tytandderwen Caravan Site ►►
Tel: (0678) 520573
Grassy 10-pitch site
Open Easter–Oct, must book Jul–Aug
Llandderfel: Bryn Melyn Caravan Site ►►
Tel: (067 83) 212
Fairly level 40-pitch site (25 tents)
Open Easter–Oct, must book public holidays
Llandrillo: Hendwr Farm Site ►►
Tel: (049 084) 210
Flat, grassy 60-pitch site (20 caravans)
Open Apr–Oct, must book Jul–Aug

Golfing
Bala:
Tel: (0678) 520359
Mountainous course, 10 holes, 4986yds, par 66, SSS64
Vale of Llangollen:
Tel: (0978) 860040
Scenic parkland course, 18 holes, 6330yds, par 70, SSS69

Riding
Llangollen:
Pengwern Mill Riding School, Pengwern Mill Farm
Tel: (0978) 860435

General
Bala: Bala Lake Railway: narrow-gauge 4½m track from Bala to Llanuwchllyn
Open Easter–mid-Oct 9–6
Chirk: Chirk Castle: 14th-century fortress with 1½m driveway
Open Apr–Oct (Wed, Thu, Sat & Sun) 2–5
Llangollen: Canal Exhibition: warehouse museum
Open Easter–Sep, daily 11–5.30
Llangollen Station: restored GWR station with rolling stock display
Open all year (Sat & Sun) 10–5
Plas Newydd: 18th-century house with oak carvings, leatherwork, exhibition room
Open May–Sep 10–7.30 (Sun 11–4)
Tel: (0978) 860234
Valle Crucis Abbey: remains of 13th-century Cistercian abbey
Open all year

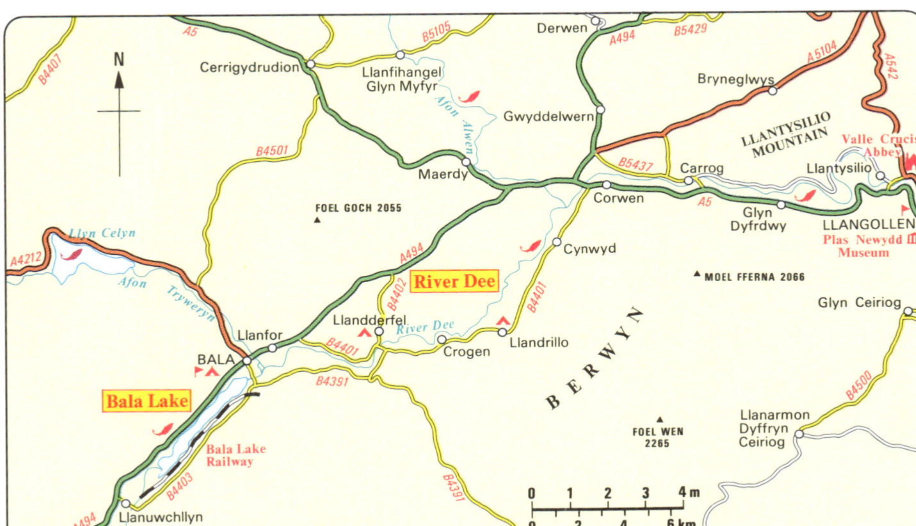

River Alwen
Dee tributary offering good trout with chances of salmon
Daily tickets: Golden Pheasant Hotel, Glyn Ceiriog or Cambrian Fly Fishery, The Old Vicarage, Trevor, Llangollen
Tel: (097 881) 2353
Water Authority: WNWDA, Cambrian Way, Brecon, Powys
Tel: (0874) 226

Llyn Celyn
Reservoir off A4212 well-stocked with small fish
Daily tickets: W E Pugh, 74 High Street, Bala
Water Authority: as River Alwen

Welsh Coast

Aberystwyth – Barmouth

Angling Associations
Aberystwyth Angling Association
Aberystwyth Sea Angling Club
Endeavour Group
New Dovey Fishery Association

Tackle Dealers
Aber Gun Supplies, 13 Terrace Road, Aberystwyth
Roderick James, Seafarer, Church Street, Barmouth
W H G Owen, High Street, Barmouth
J E Rosser, 3 Queen Street, Aberystwyth

HM Coastguard
Aberdovey: *Tel: (065 472) 327*
Aberystwyth: *Tel: (0970) 612220*

Inland Fishing Water Authority
Welsh National Water Development Authority
Tel: Brecon (0874) 3181

The mid-Wales coast tends to be overshadowed by the rugged scenery of North Gwynedd, but from an angler's point of view, Cardigan Bay and its attendant game rivers are more than a match for their northern counterparts. Numerous mountain streams offer good quality salmon and a glance at the views, whilst fishing the estuaries, may surprise those who tend to think of this region as rather ordinary when compared with the dramatic north.

Aberystwyth, the major town of Cardigan Bay, has remained largely unchanged through the 20th-century, but remains popular as a health resort due to its bracing breezes and fairly constant temperatures. The rivers Ystwyth and Rheidol join at the very last minute to swell the harbour, where bass fishing can be profitable almost all year round. Other local vantage points are Queen's Beach, the old landing stage and Tanybwlch where during the month of September, 10lb bass are not unusual. However, flatfish are not common here as the beach tends to be rather stony. Peeler crab is the best bait, but the idler anglers make do with frozen mackerel!

Inshore fishing again yields bass, plus several standard species, but it is further out to sea that Aberystwyth shows its prowess as a fishing port. The Endeavour Group, a very enterprising and helpful association, has exclusive rights to all waters beyond three miles and fishes them to the full. They make regular shark-hunting trips, taking up to twelve anglers some twenty miles out in sturdy 36-foot boats. Normally, two floats are placed behind the vessel and set from mid-water upwards (with position depending on prevailing weather conditions) is a 14-foot wire trace – the main line weight being 50lb. The porbeagle shark visits every year between July and early October, whilst the blue shark, strangely, appears only every third year – the next scheduled visits being 1983 and 1986. The headquarters of the

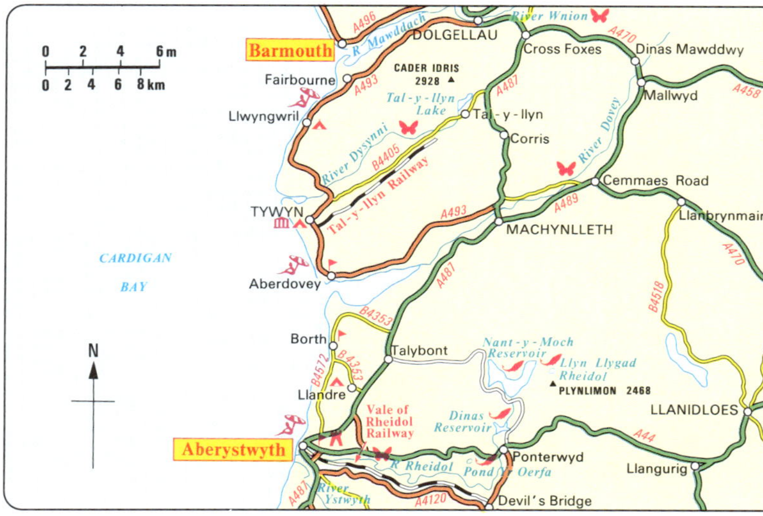

River Dovey (Dyfi)
30-mile river highly rated for sea trout, with fair chances for the visitor
Daily tickets (in advance): Dolbrawd Maeth Hall Country House Hotel, Dinas Mawddwy or E Francis, Nant Nest Stores, Dinas Mawddwy
Tel: (065 04) 215
Water Authority: WNWDA (Gwynedd River Division)
Tel: (0874) 3181

River Dysynni
Excellent for bass and mullet, plus salmon, sea and brown trout
Daily tickets (in advance): Railway Inn, Abergynolwyn
Water Authority: as River Dovey

River Rheidol
Good brown trout, plus salmon and sea trout runs, with ample access for visitors in lower reaches
Daily tickets (in advance): J E Rosser, Queen Street, Aberystwyth
Tel: (0970) 617451
Water Authority: as River Dovey except SW Wales River Division

River Wnion
A Mawddach tributary containing brown trout and some salmon, with limited chances for non-residents
Daily tickets (in advance): Celfi Diddan, Eldon Square, Dolgellau
Tel: (0341) 422388
Water Authority: as River Dovey

Ponterwyd Lakes
A group of stillwaters near to Aberystwyth containing brown and rainbow trout
Daily tickets and Water Authority: as River Rheidol

An Aberystwyth bass

Shark Club of Wales, formed in 1977, is here in Aberystwyth.

Tope enthusiasts, too, should profit from the various trips organised by the Endeavour Group. It is a fact that Aberystwyth waters yield more qualifying tope (30lb tope on no more than a 35lb line) than any other port in Europe. If turbot is your kind of fish then, again, in quantity (if not quality), Cardigan Bay is exceptionally good.

A brief word about the local River Rheidol – sewin (the local name for sea trout) are on the increase here, thanks to the breeding scheme introduced by the Aberystwyth Angling Association. In fine weather, Butcher and Coachman flies are best, but worm is advisable when the river is in spate. For stillwater specialists, just a few miles inland are the Ponterwyd Lakes, containing average-sized brown and rainbow trout. Tickets are readily available from the local tackle shops.

At Borth the beaches are much sandier and in consequence flounder and conger are good sport. Crabs and lobsters may also be taken here at certain times.

Above the village of Borth is the scenic Dovey Estuary. Arguably, this is the best salmon fishing stretch in Wales. Certainly 25-pounders have been caught here, plus plentiful, above-average sea trout. The estuary is association-controlled, with no Sunday fishing, but opportunities for the visitor are generally fairly good.

Various species, including bass, brill, plaice and sole, can be caught by draught net off Aberdovey from May to November. Bass may also be successfully fished here from anchored boats near the shore.

A few miles up-river, into the Dovey Valley, runs Pennal Stream. This brook offers small, but plentiful trout. At Machynlleth, more salmon and trout fishing may be had. Except in rough weather, only flies are permitted – the best for this stretch being Haslam and the locally-hailed Dovey Emperor. Round to the north of the estuary, with the local farmer's blessing, trout fishing is free in aptly-named and beautiful Happy Valley.

Back on up the coast, Tywyn is a good spot for mullet (at Broadwater using maggot as bait) and bass. The local River Dysynni provides fine game fishing, with sea trout in abundance during late summer and averaging 5lb.

Past Penrhyn Point is a second lovely estuary emptying into Cardigan Bay. The River Mawddach's last six miles to the sea contain large bass, flatfish and mullet, with plenty of natural bait on nearby beaches.

Inland at Dolgellau, the River Wnion offers migratory trout and salmon. The run here is from late June to September. Some eight miles to the south is Tal-y-llyn, a locally rated trout reservoir located in the shadow of Cader Idris, a starkly beautiful mountain.

The delightful old town of Barmouth has several beach and rock vantage points, but the angler should beware of the tide coming in at unusual angles. The tiny island of Ynys-y-Brawd in the harbour is a good spot for bass and flounder.

Barmouth's draw as a tourist centre is not that there are various places to visit, but the charm of the town itself. The tightly-clustered old houses are half set into the cliff and behind them various walkways lead up to Dinas Olau, a National Trust area which affords lovely views of the Mawddach Estuary. Across the quay by ferry, is Fairbourne, where a miniature railway plies the half-mile stretch of shore, a great attraction for any of the younger members of the family.

At Dolgellau are the ruins of the 700-year-old Cistercian Cymmer Abbey, but evidence of a very much earlier community here, is the intersection of three characteristically straight Roman roads at the town centre.

Tywyn is a terminus of the oldest 2ft 3in-gauge track in the world. The Tal-y-llyn railway is just over seven miles long, with three intermediate stations. It is worth the trip, if only to view the lovely Dolgoch waterfalls. Back in the town, the railway museum allows devotees to gaze at a small collection of rare locomotives and wagons.

Aberdovey is a well-sheltered resort and is consequently very popular in summer. Golfers will find the local course very appealing. The Dyfi estuary is noted for flatfish. The best spot is the Ynyslas Dunes on the south bank.

In Aberystwyth the book-worm will find The National Library of Wales an Aladdin's cave. Several rare books and manuscripts are housed here, including the only known copies of the first book printed in Welsh. The 13th-century Aberystwyth Castle ruins have been pleasantly set amongst public gardens, and on a clear day the distant peaks of Snowdon can be seen from the castle rock.

Speaking of rocks, whether you like to angle from rocks, beach, boat or bank, a sojourn at the northern coastline of Cardigan Bay should provide many hours of good sport.

Camping
Llandre: Riverside Park ►►►
Tel: (097 087) 682
Level site 4m NE of Aberystwyth
Open Easter and Jun–Sep, no bookings
Llwyngwril: Gwril Caravan Site ►►
Tel: (034 16) 431
Flat 40-pitch site (no tents)
Open Easter–Sep, no bookings
Tywyn: Woodlands Holiday Park ►►►
Tel: (0654) 710471
Attractive 20-pitch site (no tents)
Open Apr–Oct, must book

Golfing
Aberdovey:
Tel: (065 472) 210
Lovely seaside course, 18 holes, 6421yds, par 71, SSS71
Aberystwyth:
Tel: (0970) 2691
Rolling meadowland course, 18 holes, 5735yds, par 67, SSS68
Borth & Ynslas:
Tel: (097 081) 202
Windy seaside links, 18 holes, 5992yds, par 70, SSS70

Walking Trails
Dinas Olau: various steep hillside walks through Britain's very first National Trust property. Start from any point along the old High Street, Barmouth

General
Aberystwyth:
Aberystwyth Castle: 13th-century ruins
Open all year
National Library of Wales: impressive number of books, prints, MSS & drawings
Open all year (ex Sun)
Tel: (0970) 3816/9
Dolgellau: Cymmer Abbey: remains of 13th-century monastery
Open all year
Tywyn: Narrow-Gauge Railway Museum: small collection of locomotives & wagons
Open Easter–Oct, plus winter by arrangement
Tel: (0654) 710472
Tal-y-llyn Railway: oldest 2ft 3in-gauge railway in the world, steam-operated on 7¼m track
Daily service Easter–Sep
Tel: (0654) 710472

Angler's Directory for Wales and West Midlands

Clubs and Associations

Aberystwyth Angling Association, PO Box 15, Aberystwyth, Dyfed

Aberystwyth Sea Angling Club (The Secretary), Wynchmore Cafe, Clarach, Aberystwyth, Dyfed

Bala & District Angling Association (E J Leary), Sarnau, Mount Street, Bala, Gwynedd
Tel: (0678) 520248

Birmingham Angling Association (The Secretary), 40 Thorpe Street, Birmingham, West Midlands

Cheshire Angling Association, (F James), 43 Sweet Briar Crescent, Crewe, Cheshire

Crewe Pioneers, (A Meyler), 11 Lingfield Drive, Crewe, Cheshire

Endeavour Group, (V Haig), Schooner's Landing, Aberystwyth, Dyfed
Tel: (0970) 612818

Hereford & District Angling Association (H Webb), 96 East Street, Hereford

Liverpool and District Angling Association (J Johnson), 97 Liverpool Road North, Magull, Liverpool, Merseyside

Llangollen Angling Association (S I Evans), The Dingle, Abbey Road, Llangollen, Clwyd

Llanuwchllyn Angling Club (H E Morris), Plas Newydd, Llanuwychllyn, Gwynedd

Maelor Angling Association (N I Wright), 34 Heol Cefnydd, Cefn Mawr, Ruabon, Clwyd
Tel: (0978) 821040

Montgomeryshire Angling Association (S J Harding), 29 Rhoslan, Guilsfield, Welshpool, Powys
Tel: (0938) 3303

New Dovey Fishery Association, (D M Jones), Hengoed, Plas Machynlleth, Powys
Tel: (0654) 2073

Ross-on-Wye Angling Club (V R Hepburn), 30 Claytons Bridstow, Ross-on-Wye, Hereford and Worcester
Tel: (0989) 4255

Sabrina Angling Club (W G Smart), Sunny Hill Lyth Bank, Bayston Hill, Shrewsbury, Salop
Tel: (074 372) 2237

Warrington Angling Association (J Jackson), 23 Nora Street, Warrington, Lancashire

Tackle Shops

Aberystwyth
Aberystwyth Sports Centre, 60 North Parade
Tel: (0970) 617565
E L Reddington, 23 Chalybeate Street
J Rosser, 3 Queen Street
Tel: (0970) 617451

Bala
R E Evans, Bradford House
W E Pugh, 74 High Street
Tel: (0678) 520248

Barmouth
All Sports, Beach Road
Tel: (0341) 280240

Evesham
Evesham Sports Centre, 60a Bridge Street
Tel: (0386) 3883
J Heritage, Boat Lane
Tel: (0386) 3278

Hereford
H Hatton, 73 St Owen Street
Tel: (0432) 2317
B Thorpe, Fishery Dept, Broad Street
Tel: (0432) 6202

Llangollen
Cambrian Fly Fishery, The Old Vicarage, Trevor
Tel: (097 881) 2353

Machynlleth
T Aylward, Maengwyn Street
Tel: (0654) 2438

Ross-on-Wye
G & B Sports, 19 High Street
Tel: (0989) 3723

Shrewsbury
Ebrall Bros, Smithfield Road
Tel: (0743) 3048
G Forrest, 12 Baker Street
Tel: (0743) 56878

Stratford-upon-Avon
A C Claridge, Greenhill Street
Tel: (0789) 292778

Welshpool
A E Bond, Hall Street
Tel: (0938) 3327
C D Millington, 3 Church Street

Water Authorities

Severn Trent Water Authority, Abelson House, 2297 Coventry Road, Sheldon, Birmingham, West Midlands
Tel: (021 743) 4222
and 64 Albert Road North, Malvern, Hereford and Worcester
Tel: (068 45) 61511

Welsh National Water Development Authority, Cambrian Way, Brecon, Powys
Tel: (0874) 3181

Hotels and Inns

Alcester
Fish Hotel, Wixford
Tel: (078 988) 2478

Bala
Plas Coch
Tel: (0248) 714272
White Lion
Tel: (0678) 520230
Ye Old Bull's Head
Tel: (0678) 520438

Corwen
Owain Glyndwr Hotel

Hereford
Longworth Hall Hotel, Lugwardine
Tel: (0432) 850223

Llangollen
Golden Pheasant, Glyn Ceiriog
Tel: (069 172) 281

Ross-on-Wye
Pengethley Hotel
Tel: (098 987) 211

Shrewsbury
Wingfield Arms
Tel: (0743) 850750

Stratford-upon-Avon
Salmon Tail Hotel
Tel: (0789) 297765

Symond's Yat
Saracen's Head

Tywyn
Corbett Arms

Welshpool
Black Lion
Westwood Park Hotel
Tel: (0938) 3327

North of England

4

Lake District

Water Authority
North West Water Authority
Tel: Warrington (0925) 53999
Salmon, migratory trout, and brown trout/coarse fish licences issued for periods of one year and seven days (salmon licences also available for part-year from June 1)
Postal applications to: Finance Department, NWWA, Rivers Division, PO Box 12, New Town House, Buttermarket Street, Warrington
Licences available from many tackle shops, tourist offices and village agents

Angling Associations
Calder Angling Association
Egremont Angling Association
Gosforth Angling Association
Keswick Anglers' Association
Penrith Angling Association
Windermere, Ambleside and District Angling Association

Tackle shops (and other day ticket and permit sources)
Esthwaite Estates Ltd, Estate Office, Hawkshead
The Gun Shop, Lorton Road, Cockermouth
P Musgrave & Sons Ltd, Lake Road, Bowness
National Trust NW Region Office, Borrans Road, Ambleside
NWWA Eastern Division, Talbot Road, Old Trafford, Manchester
South Lakeland District Council, Recreation Department, Windermere
South Lakeland Fishing Tackle, Kirkland, Kendal
[Plus many other sources]

Close Seasons
Salmon: November 1 – January 31 **except:** River Eden and all rivers and lakes tributary or connected to the river: October 15 – January 14
Rivers and connected lakes Annas, Bleng, Irt, Esk, Mite, Calder, Ehen: November 1 – March 31
Rivers and connected lakes Derwent, Ellen, Waver, Wampool: November 1 – February 14
Sea trout: October 16 – April 30 **except:** Rivers and connected lakes Annas, Bleng, Esk, Mite, Calder, Ehen: November 1 – April 30
Brown trout and *char:* October 1 – March 14
Coarse fish: March 15 – June 15

While the Pennines form a jagged backbone to England's north country, they do not have the dramatic grandeur of the Cumbrian Mountains or the contrast between the still depths of remote lakes pooled in valleys below soaring peaks. The Lake District is perhaps England's only true mountain country, founded on age-old volcanic rocks scoured and rent by wild weather, glaciers and raging waters. It is a paradise for walkers, anglers, campers and all who love the great outdoors.

Surpassed only by the West Country, this second most popular leisure area in Britain also offers a host of attractions for less active visitors. It is country in which the National Trust owns large holdings, particularly around the lakes themselves, with many beautiful gardens to see and waterside spots at which to picnic and while away a few pleasant hours.

Anglers have an absolutely phenomenal choice of points for fishing from both shore and boat, many of the lakes being free of charge to holders of the mandatory North West Water Authority Licence. There are superb trout and salmon streams, too, where club and hotel interests hold waters which are also readily available to visitors seeking daily or weekly tickets.

In this survey of the unique angling opportunities in the area, the sixteen main lakes and the associated river and tarn waters are discussed separately; the southern lakes west of Windermere first, and the northern lakes west of Ullswater and the Haweswater Reservoir on pages 60 and 61.

Windermere
This island-studded lake is about ten miles long and is the largest sheet of still freshwater in England. Around the north west end of the lake are extensive National Trust holdings

which offer free bank fishing and some opportunities for small boat launching. Users of boats should note that powered craft must be registered and there are a number of special regulations governing small craft (full details can be obtained at Tourist Information centres). Other launch points are at Bowness (the lake's main town), Waterhead and Ambleside, which also offer boat hire.

Windermere is a noted water for big trout of up to 8lb, perch, pike and the hard-fighting char. This beautiful fish is best caught when deep-trolled lures are used. Locally the char is considered a great delicacy and it is fished on a semi-commercial basis.

At its southern end, Windermere runs to the sea by the River Leven, a water which fishes well for salmon, sea trout and some coarse fish.

Tickets to fish the Leven are available from the Swan Hotel, Newby Bridge.

Grasmere and Rydal Water
Much of the land surrounding Grasmere, a mile-long water with good access from the A591, is owned by the National Trust and fishing the lake is free. The water is, however, bounded by some private properties and it is necessary to obtain the owner's permission in some spots. Power boats are not allowed on this lake and launching of small craft is limited to the boat hire yard at Pavement End, Grasmere. Brown trout, perch and pike (a recent introduction to the lakes as a whole) are the main species. Fishing on nearby Rydal Water is controlled by the Windermere, Ambleside and District Angling Association and permits can be obtained from several local shops and tourist offices. The club also controls trout fishing on the River Brathay whose waters feeds these two linked lakes.

Esthwaite Water
Near to the Beatrix Potter village of Far Sawrey (reached by ferry across Windermere from Bowness), Esthwaite is owned by Esthwaite Estates Limited, which issues permits for fishing the lake's perch, pike and brown trout from Hawkshead Post Office and The Village Shop, Far Sawrey.

Coniston Water
One of the most famous of all the lakes, Coniston is a tranquil five-mile long lake surrounded on all sides by stunning mountain scenery, dominated to the north west by Coniston Old Man's 2 663-foot stature. Like Grasmere, Coniston is surrounded by many National Trust properties and fishing is free – again, there are many private water's edge lands and you should enquire thoroughly about access. Boats are available at the Coniston Boating Centre near to the village. Launch facilities are provided here, at a car park at the lake's north end, and at Beck Leven Foot (permission from Brantwood Estate).

Coniston's deepest water is in the middle reaches. Here it is even possible to reach the char's favourite deepwater grounds by a cast from the bank. However, the predominant catches are again perch, pike and trout.

Wastwater
Deep in the highest part of the Cumbrian Mountains, remote Wastwater is the source of the River Irt and is reached only by narrow lanes from the A595 coast road. Permits to fish the lake's perch, pike and trout are available from The Warden of the National Trust-owned Wasdale Head campsite (tents only). A more attractive proposition is the River Irt, which is locally famed for its good run of salmon and sea trout. While much of the river is fishable only by members of the Millom & District Angling Association, there are ticket facilities on a stretch at Wasdale (Gosforth Angling Association) and near Drigg (Lutwidge Arms Hotel, Holmrook).

Yew Tree Tarn, near Coniston

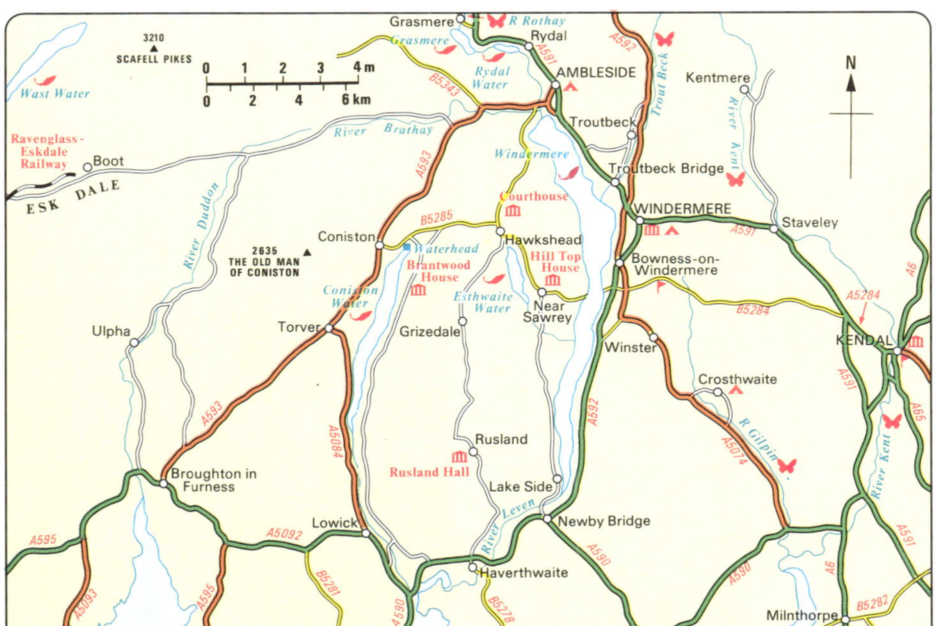

River Gilpin
Small salmon stream with some chances for visitors
Daily tickets: Northern Angling Association (G Wilson), 11 Guildford Avenue, Chorley, Lancashire
Tel: (025 72) 65905
Water Authority: NWWA, New Town House, Buttermarket Street, Warrington, Cheshire
Tel: (0925) 53999

River Kent
A good, but largely private, game river with limited chances
Daily tickets: E Atkinson, Strickland Gate, Kendal, Cumbria
Tel: (0539) 20300

River Rothay
Almost exclusively trout fishing
Daily tickets: P Musgrave & Son, Lake Road, Bowness, Cumbria
Water Authority: as River Gilpin

Trout Beck
Fast-flowing perch and trout stream
Daily tickets: Windermere, Ambleside and District Angling Club (R T Parry), Yewbank, Clappersgate, Ambleside, Cumbria
Tel: (096 63) 3512
Water Authority: as River Gilpin

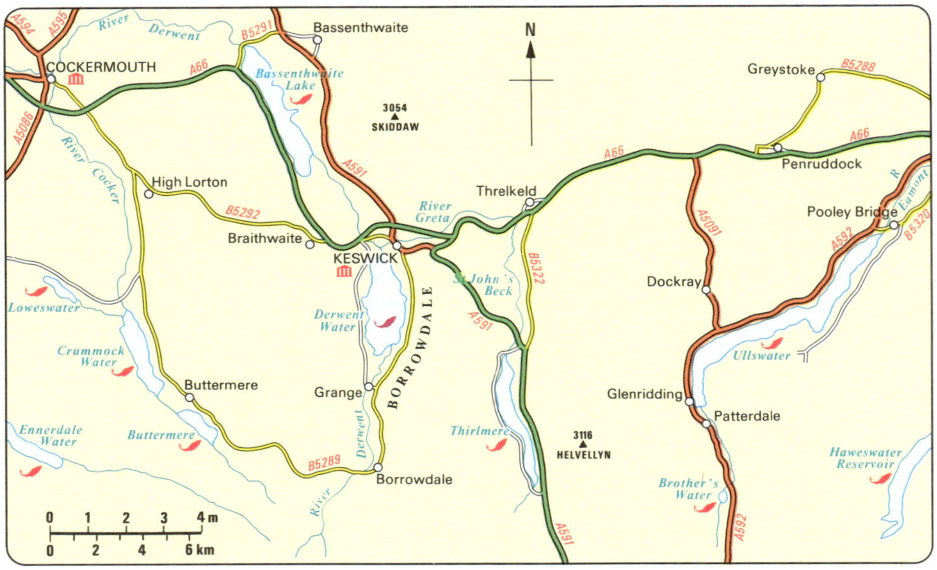

Haweswater
It is in the northern lakes of Haweswater and Ullswater that the elusive schelly is found. Closely related to the gwyniad of Bala Lake, this herring-like fish is in fact a salmonid and, like its Welsh cousin, is rarely taken on rod and line. The record schelly (or skelly) is a 1lb 10oz specimen taken in Ullswater, but this fish is occasionally found in the NWWA-controlled reservoir. A limited number of permits to fish for trout by fly are issued by the authority (also enabling anglers to fish the Wet Sleddale Reservoir) and written applications are required. Haweswater Beck, flowing from the lake to the Lowther, has some permit fishing (brown trout and char) available from the Crown and Mitre Inn, Bampton Grange.

Ullswater and Brother's Water
Ullswater and its nearby linked Brother's Water can both be fished free for pike, perch, brown trout and schelly. For Ullswater there is a boat hire yard at Glenridding at the south end of the water. Do check with local sources about bankside access however, as many private properties dot the shore.

Fishing this giant lake (eight miles long and covering an area of 2 200 acres) is not easy, as the waters vary considerably and can be up to 200 feet deep. The trout run very big and a fish of 8lb is on the cards for anglers using deep-fished lures from boats. Perch and trout provide the sport at the tiny Brother's Water which does not rival the size of Ullswater's specimens, although it can be fished on days when Ullswater seems like a dead lake. The River Eamont connects Ullswater to the Eden and fly-fishing-only permits to the upper waters may be obtained from Penrith Angling Association.

Thirlmere
Lying to the west of the glowering peak of Helvellyn, Thirlmere has heavily-wooded banks and has become a reservoir for Manchester. Fishing is controlled by the NWWA and there are a limited number of permits available for applicants in writing.

Derwentwater
The lake immortalised on crayon boxes and the water which sits on the doorstep of Keswick, is Derwentwater. Largely controlled by the Keswick Anglers' Association, the waters hold good stocks of trout, pike and perch as well as having a salmon run from late May. Tickets are available from several local tackle shops and there is a boat hire centre at Manor Road, Keswick. The lake also has several launch points for small craft (note there is a 10mph speed limit on powered boats). The River Derwent flows through the lake to Bassenthwaite and salmon, sea trout and trout permits can be obtained for some stretches by application in advance (Keswick Anglers' Association).

Bassenthwaite Lake
Owned by the Lake District Special Planning Board, Bassenthwaite Lake, north of Derwentwater on the River Derwent, can be fished with locally obtained permits. The lake has good stocks of brown trout, perch and pike and has a fair salmon run. Most local rods troll with minnow for the best fish. The riparian owners' permission is required for boat launching and no powered craft are allowed.

Buttermere
Trout, perch and pike teem in Buttermere, a lake surrounded by extensive National Trust holdings. Permits, issued by this organisation are available at local tackle dealers in Cockermouth and Buttermere. Small boat launching is permitted (access from the B5289) with National Trust permission.

Crummock Water and Loweswater
Connected by the headwaters of the River Cocker, Crummock Water and Loweswater lie between Buttermere and Cockermouth. Crummock Water is quite deep and has a good salmon run – fish that are usually caught by deep trolling. Loweswater is a shallower lake and has no char although it shares trout, pike and perch in good numbers with Crummock Water. There is a boat hire facility on Loweswater at Kirkstile Inn where permits for Buttermere, Crummock Water and Loweswater may also be purchased. The Inn also gives permission for boat launchings on the three lakes (no

power boats are allowed on Crummock Water).

Ennerdale Water
Fishing on this most westerly of the lakes is controlled by the Calder Angling Association and only a limited number of permits are available by written application. The lake does hold considerable stocks of trout and char and the best months for trout are undoubtedly May, June and July. The lake is the source of the River Ehen, which has a good run of salmon and sea trout. Fishing on the river is controlled by Egremont Angling Association and the Wath Brow and Ennerdale Angling Association, both of which offer a limited number of permits. Some riparian owners also offer some fishing on the river.

Many families who want to enjoy the Lake District to the full will choose the outdoor life and the area certainly has lots to offer campers. While most of the facilities cluster around the major tourist havens of Windermere (there are superb sites around Ambleside, Bowness and the lake's southern end) Ullswater also has its sites. Keswick and Cockermouth are other camping centres with better access to the northern lakes and the north west coast.

As befits this rugged country, the Lakes form a gigantic outdoor leisure complex. It has to be said that some of the more popular tourist spots are totally traffic-bound at peak times. So what better way to see the countryside than by hiring a bicycle? There are centres in Cockermouth, Keswick, Kendal, Bowness and Ambleside. Another more gentle means of transport is to explore the fells and woods on horseback. Over forty riding and pony-trekking stables in the area offer horses for hire by the hour or day as well as guiding half-day and day trekking parties. If you want to put in a bit of practice for your winter break there is even a grass-ski-ing centre complete with ski-lift and instructors based at one of the campsites, Limefitt Park near Ambleside.

But it is the chance of treading the paths once walked by the Lakeland poets, painters and writers – Coleridge, Ruskin, Southey, Beatrix Potter and, of course, Wordsworth – that inspires many visitors. The district is laced with signed walks and a network of long-established footpaths to suit idle strollers and mile-eating fell-walkers alike. Most of the major lakes can be circumnavigated on foot with no more special equipment than a pair of stout shoes. If you venture to high ground take warm clothing, a map and a compass as the fells are noted for rapid weather changes.

This is a land of little railways, too. From a station at Lakeside, which connects to the Sealink steamers plying Windermere, you can ride the Lakeside and Haverthwaite Railway through the beautiful valley of the Leven. It is a three and a half-mile track ending at the line's rolling stock workshop and exhibition. The Ravenglass and Eskdale Railway is a former slate-carrying line running seven miles from the coast up Eskdale. While Windermere has the best developed water transport, most of the other major lakes have boat hire centres.

Many families heading for the Lakes neglect the fact that the coast is within easy striking distance of the major centres. South, from Grange-over-Sands at the head of Morecambe Bay around the narrow headland of Haws Point near Barrow and north to Maryport and Beckfoot are some superb beaches, small unspoiled resorts and, if the anglers want a change, some fine sea fishing venues.

It is just this kind of contrast between sea, lake, mountain and forest that has fostered the Lake District's undeniable appeal to lovers of the British countryside of all ages.

Camping
Ambleside: Low Wray National Trust Campsite ►►
Attractive 206-pitch site (no caravans)
Open Easter–Oct, no bookings
Bouth: Black Beck Caravan Park ►
Tel: (022 986) 274
Quiet 45-pitch site (20 tents)
Open Mar–Oct, must book
Crosthwaite: Lambhowe Caravan Park ►
Tel: (044 88) 483
Pretty 10-pitch site (no tents)
Open Apr–Oct, must book Jul–Aug
Windermere: Limefitt Park ►►►►►
Tel: (096 63) 2300
Large 345-pitch site
Open Apr–Oct, should book
Park Cliffe Farm Caravan & Camping Site ►►►
Tel: (0448) 31344
Partly sloping 250-pitch site (no caravans)
Open Easter–Oct, should book Jul–Aug

Golfing
Bowness: Windermere
Tel: (096 62) 3123
Short, upland course with fine views, 18 holes, 4940yds, par 67, SSS65
Kendal:
Tel: (0539) 24079
Moorland course, 18 holes, 5483yds, par 66, SSS67

Riding
Windermere: Wynlass Beck Stables (W M Oakden)
Tel: (096 62) 3811

Walking Trails
Belle Isle: 2m (¾hr) lakeland walk. Start from Belle Isle Boat Service, Bowness Promenade
Brantwood Nature Trail: 3¼m (2hr) signposted, scenic lakeland walk. Start from Brantwood House, Coniston Water
Millwood Forest Nature Trail: 1m (½hr) walk within the Wildlife Centre, Grizedale
Tel: (022 984) 273

General
Ambleside: Stagshaw Gardens: delightful woodland garden with wide range of shrubs
Open all year
Bowness: Graythwaite Hall Gardens: 7-acre landscaped gardens
Open Apr–Jun daily 10–6
Hill Top: 17th-century house, home of Beatrix Potter
Open Apr–Oct daily (ex Fri)
Tel: (096 66) 334
Coniston: Brantwood: home of John Ruskin, deer trails within grounds
Open Easter–mid-Oct daily (ex Mon & Tue)
Hawkshead: Courthouse: remains of pre-Reformation priory, housing museum & craft exhibits
Open Easter then May–Oct daily (ex Mon) 2–5
Kendal: Abbot Hall Art Gallery: various exhibits within fine 18th-century house
Open all year (Sat & Sun afternoons only)
Tel: (0539) 22464
Kendal Museum: extensive natural history & archaeology exhibits
Open all year (Sat & Sun afternoons only)
Tel: (0539) 21374
Rusland: Rusland Hall: 17th/18th-century house containing unusual antiques and mechanical instruments
Open Apr–Sep daily 11–6
Tel: (022 984) 276
Windermere: Lake District National Park Centre: 19th-century house in 32-acre grounds with audio-visual displays, films, picnic areas
Open mid-Mar–mid-Nov 10 onwards
Tel: (096 62) 2231
Steamboat Museum: unusual collection of 19th-century vessels
Open Easter–Oct 10–5 (Sun 2–5)
Tel: (096 62) 5565

Calf Close Bay, Derwentwater

River Ure

Aysgarth – Boroughbridge

Water Authority
Yorkshire Water Authority
Two types of rod licence issued: salmon, sea-trout, brown trout, freshwater fish and eels throughout authority area, licence issued for season, seven-day and day periods. To fish rivers north of, and including the Esk, a limited licence is available for season or seven-day periods
YWA: *Tel: (0532) 448201*

Angling Associations
Boroughbridge and District Angling Association
Knaresborough Piscatorial Society
Leeds and District Amalgamated Society of Anglers
Ripon Piscatorial Society
Thornaby Angling Association
Wensleydale Angling Association

Tackle dealers and other sources of licences and permits
Blue Lion, East Witton
Brewers Arms, 2 Bondgate, Ripon
M H and C Johnson, Briggate, Knaresborough
Newby Hall Estate, The Lodges, Skelton-on-Ure
Old Horn Inn, Spennithorne
Palmer Flatt Hotel, Aysgarth
Rose & Crown Hotel, Bainbridge
Three Horseshoes, Boroughbridge
B Wain, 82 Bondgate, Ripon
All in North Yorkshire

Close Seasons
Note YWA close seasons differ considerably from those of other water authorities:
Salmon and *sea trout:* November 1 – April 5, *brown trout:* October 1 – March 24, *coarse fish:* February 28 – May 31

Yorkshire's River Ure rises in the wild Pennine fells of the Yorkshire-Cumbria border and runs almost directly east, gathering strength from dozens of tiny hillside becks in the picturesque setting of Wensleydale. In its upper reaches the Ure is a rocky, forceful, little stream fished locally for trout, but at Aysgarth the river tumbles dramatically over a series of falls to become a serious fishing river swollen by the major contribution of the Bishopdale Beck waters. Ignominiously, this fine river which takes in the hill towns of Masham and Middleham (famed as race-horse stabling centres) and the majesty of Ripon, loses its name below Boroughbridge to become (with the waters of the Swale and Nidd) the Yorkshire Ouse. This river also changes name still later to become the mighty Humber.

Just above Aysgarth, at Bainbridge, is the first of the Ure's ticketed waters, a six-mile stretch amid scenery that is counted among Yorkshire's best. The Wensleydale Angling Association control the water and some tickets are obtainable locally. In the Aysgarth area there are two main sets of falls and below the first drop are waters for which tickets can be obtained from the Palmer Flatt Hotel. Brown trout are fairly small here but there is also the chance to take grayling.

Below this section the waters are guarded jealously by local clubs and estates and it is downstream from the next set of falls that the river opens up again and coarse fishing really starts. From the Redmire Falls the river is noted for dace and chub fishing and from Wensley, at the mouth of the Dale, barbel, too, begin to make their presence felt.

The first opportunities for visitors to sample this sport begin at the Iron Bridge in the race-horse town of Middleham. A collection of holdings stretch from here down to East Witton through Ulshaw Bridge, Kilgrimbridge and Spennithorne. Some are controlled by the mighty Leeds and District Amalgamated Society of Anglers offering day tickets through the Old Horn Inn at Spennithorne, while other reaches are controlled by the Thornaby Angling Association who will issue permits to postal applicants.

The river here is much wider and runs fairly deep. The fishing is superb but the fish can be very shy and it is no place for heavy tackle and the careless angler. Chub, dace, grayling and roach can be found but fish with fine lines and keep well off the skyline or your bag will be totally bare.

At Spennithorne Bridge the river has changed character again to a fast-flowing, boulder-strewn bottom – waters in which trout thrive and which offers challenging sport.

The River Cover joins the Ure near East Witton and there is a permit stretch here for which tickets are issued by the Blue Lion, East Witton. Chub, roach and dace make up most of the catches but perch make an appearance and the grayling are still present. Local rods are fond of trotting a stick float down the deeper swims, especially those with a lot of overhanging trees or bushes.

Below East Witton, the Ure skirts the ruins of historic Jervaulx Abbey to the brewery town of Masham where Theakston brew that strangest beer of all, 'Old Peculier', a name derived from that of a mediaeval court which sat in the town. Masham to Tanfield is considered to be the best trout reach of the Ure and unfortunately there are only facilities for guests of the members of the many clubs which control the waters.

From the cathedral city of Ripon the waters become a better prospect for visitors. As the river finds its way through Ripon it changes from deep to shallow runs several times and visitors are advised to seek advice from local tackle shops about the best stands. To add to difficulties the river becomes navigable at the racecourse and there has been a considerable increase in boat traffic over the last few years. Chub, roach, trout, grayling, dace, pike, barbel and perch abound in these reaches with chub and dace being the predominant species for autumn fishing. Barbel are more apparent during the summer months.

Seven miles of the Ure from the Ure Bank caravan site north of the town down to the Newby Hall estate can be fished on day tickets

Trout fly fishing on the Ure near Wensley

Camping
Leyburn: Akebar Park ►►►
Tel: (0677) 50201
Partly sloping 110-pitch site (50 tents)
Open Easter–Oct, must book Jul–Aug
Ripon: Sleningford Water Mill ►►►
Tel: (0765) 85201
Level 65-pitch site (25 caravans)
Open mid-May–Oct, book for caravans
Ure Bank Tourist Caravan Site ►►►
Tel: (0765) 2964
Well-kept 199-pitch site (24 tents)
Open Mar–Oct, must book Jul–Aug

Golfing
Ripon City:
Tel: (0765) 3640
Hard walking parkland course, 9 holes, 5780yds, par 70, SSS68

Riding
Boroughbridge: Prospect Stables, Prospect Villa, Minskip
Tel: (090 12) 2791

Walking Trails
Aysgarth Mini Nature Trail: ¾m (1hr) circular walk including waterfall. Start from Aysgarth National Park Centre car park off A684 by Palmer Flatts Hotel

General
Aysgarth: The Old Mill: a museum of horse-drawn vehicles
Open Easter–Oct 10–12 & 1.30–6
Tel: (0748) 3325
Leyburn: Constable Burton Hall Gardens: extensive shrubberies amid trees, small lake
Open Apr–Jul daily 9–6
Tel: (0677) 50428
Middleham: Middleham Castle: 12th-century fortress with two-storeyed keep
Open all year
Reeth: Swaledale Folk Museum: interesting local exhibits
Open Easter–Sep daily 10.30–6
Ripon: Fountains Abbey & Studley Royal Country Park: large deer park with numerous walks, plus imposing Cistercian abbey ruins
Open all year, times vary
Tel: (076 586) 639

obtained in the town (B Wain, 82 Bondgate and the Brewers Arms, 2 Bondgate). The length above North Bridge is a stretch worth tackling first as it regularly produces big weights, but from North Bridge down to Hewith Bridge the coarse fishing continues to be good. In this reach the River Skell joins the Ure and, where the Ure is carrying the extra water, chub are the main sport. Newby Hall itself offers tickets for a one-mile reach below the weir, available from the Estate Office, Skelton-on-Ure. The weir pool holds some big barbel but the bottom is very rough and tackle losses can be high.

In the final stretches of the Ure, under the A1 trunk road to Boroughbridge, are the last chances to enjoy this great little river's sport. The town is by-passed for boats by a canalised stretch leaving the water undisturbed for a chance at the occasional bream landed here – a session with ledger tackle could pay dividends. Tickets to the left bank are sold by M H and C Johnson, Briggate, Knaresborough and the Three Horseshoes, Boroughbridge. From the cricket pitch to Hall Arm Lane tickets are available but for weekdays only from Boroughbridge Post Office.

Wensleydale is at the heart of the Yorkshire Dales, the valleys running down from the Pennines draining the upper slopes to the plain of York and Selby. Campsites abound in the area from the more civilised Ure Bank site at Ripon to pitches in the wild country around Leyburn and Redmire.

Leyburn itself is an old market town perched above the Ure and it makes a good walking centre. The Shawl is a nearby two-mile long limestone scar with signed walks and views of the Dale. At Constable Burton the Hall has gardens open to the public, an informal display of alpine borders, roses and walks among a mass of fine trees.

The Dales are a National Park centred on Aysgarth and around this village are signed walks including a riverside trail past the stepped rocks of the Aysgarth falls. The water is particularly dramatic after periods of rain. The village also houses the Old Mill Museum of carriages and horse-drawn vehicles.

If you like exploring towns, Ripon must be on your list. An open market, lots of small specialist shops and the cathedral are special attractions. Here the Wakeman still blows his 9 o'clock horn as the curfew bells are rung from the Minster tower. Four miles south west of the town is Fountains Abbey, one of the best preserved (and once the richest) of the many local mediaeval retreats. The Abbey is floodlit at night and is best reached on foot through the deer-roamed grounds of Studley Royal Country Park – the very essence of romance!

The countryside of Wensleydale is still for the most part free from the seasonal pressures of the tourist hordes and it is ideal short-break and weekending country. If such a holiday can be combined with the pleasures of fishing the Ure's charming waters, so much the better.

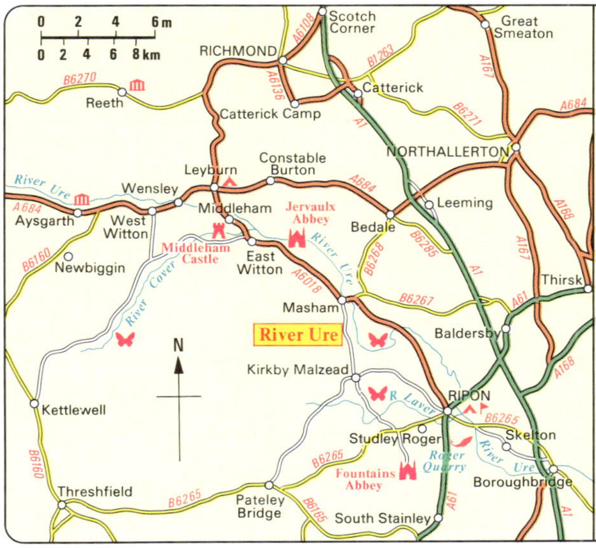

River Cover
A Ure tributary offering mixed fishing, with some opportunities for the visitor
Daily tickets: Coverbridge Inn, Middleham or East Witton Estate Office (riparian owner), Leyburn
Tel: (0969) 3109
Water Authority: YWA, West Riding House, 67 Albion Street, Leeds
Tel: (0532) 448201

River Laver
8-mile trout stream joining the Ure at Ripon
Daily tickets: R C Hodgson, 7 Queen Street, Ripon
Tel: (0765) 3029
Water Authority: as River Cover

Rogers Quarry
Gravel pit near Ripon holding coarse fish
Weekly tickets: B Wain, 82 Bondgate, Ripon
Water Authority: as River Cover

North Yorkshire Coast

Bridlington – Whitby

Angling Associations
Danby & District Angling Club
Derwent Angling Club
Esk Fishery Association
Northern Federation of Sea Angling Clubs

Tackle Dealers
Blue Star Angling Supplies, Dock End, Whitby
Buckley's Angling Supplies, 6 Leading Post Street, Scarborough
Filey Fishing Tackle, 12 Hope Street, Filey
Linford's Fishing Tackle, 12 Hilderthorpe Road, Bridlington
Pritchard's, 56 Eastborough, Scarborough
Whitby Angling Supplies, 56 Haggersgate, Whitby

HM Coastguard
Bridlington: *Tel: (0262) 72317*
Filey: *Tel: (0723) 513226*
Scarborough: *Tel: (0723) 72323*

Inland Fishing Water Authority
Yorkshire Water Authority
Tel: Leeds (0532) 448201

One of Britain's foremost sea angling areas, the coast from Bridlington, north to Whitby, is also a shore of great scenic grandeur, the line at which the bleak North Yorkshire Moors tumble into the North Sea. This is a coast that lays claim to the two highest cliffs in England, at Boulby and Ravenscar. It is strung with the remains of early settlements which mark it as a Viking invasion route and it has a wealth of seafaring traditions, from the smugglers of Robin Hood's bay to the graving of Captain Cook's ship *Endeavour* at Whitby. This historic shore can be as unforgiving as it is rewarding to the visiting angler.

Rock marks take their toll of tackle, but it is to these peaks and reefs of the sea bed that the angler should look if he wants to catch fish of any quality and quantity. Many visitors make the mistake of fishing too light. The key is to make the tackle strong and simple – a single paternoster with a weak ledger link (locally called a 'rotten bottom') is all that is required. The combination of fish-rich rocks and kelp beds along the whole of this coast means that lines of 60lb breaking strain are needed in many places.

Bridlington, one of Yorkshire's three Meccas for boat fishermen, offers tremendous scope. Traditional Yorkshire cobbles can be hired with skippers who have a lifetime's experience of finding the famed rock ledges off Flamborough Head, five miles away The resort's sandy beaches do, however, provide good codling, but only when the visitors have gone home – autumn and deep winter, after a storm, is the best time.

There is a plentiful local supply of bait – mussel, lugworm and crab can be gathered or bought from local tackle shops.

Flamborough is the focal point for fishing in this part of the coast. Big shoals of codling gather close to shore along with large plaice, conger, ling, haddock, turbot, mackerel and whiting. Remember that the spring tides here are a force to be reckoned with and hefty weights are often needed to stay on the bottom. Cobbles usually put out from the Head's North Landing, while the sheltered sandy bay of the South Landing is a more attractive proposition for the dinghy angler. Cliff-top fishing into the heavy kelp beds is a heady experience and prime cod are taken this way practically all year.

But if you have no experience of the Head, take extreme care on the chalky heights – spiked boots are sensible.

Between Flamborough and the holiday and angling centre of Scarborough there are many productive rocky shore venues, the tactics and the species being the same. Filey and its famous rock, Brigg, is a spot worth a visit, but anglers have long beach walk to reach it and unless they wait out the tide, the escape is by a metal cliff ladder.

From this point it is easy to reach deep water, but really stout tackle is essential as the sea bed is splintered.

Winter cod are the main catch and flatfish can be taken in the summer. Lugworm and crab baits can be found nearby.

Further north, the seaside resort of Scarborough, more grand than its 'fish and chip' image evokes, gives anglers plenty of boat and shore sport. Numerous charter boats ply from the sheltered harbour and close to the resort's main attractions are several marks for those who are shorebound.

The west and east piers, Marine Drive, South Bay and Cornelian Bay produce plenty of fish all year round with the bigger catches being taken in autumn and winter.

Robin Hood's Bay, where the marine life is interesting enough to have attracted a university laboratory, is a picturesque setting from which to fish the inshore rocks. Towering 600ft cliffs are the background to waters which yield plenty of big cod.

Only a few miles away is that gem of the North Yorks coast, Whitby. This old fishing port on the Esk estuary, a medley of Edwardian elegance and centuries-old fishing tradition, is a thriving boat angling centre. So popular are the boats out of Whitby that booking in advance is a must for peak period visitors – but if rough seas or full boats stop you getting afloat, the shore is also very interesting. The long arms of the east and west harbour piers are attractive venues for mackerel and flatfish during summer and for deep-shouldered codling in winter.

Charter skippers from Whitby know where to find the deep wrecks for some really stirring tussles with big ling, cod and conger. Around the Abbey steps are some bait sellers, or you can gather your own in the harbour.

Wherever you centre your stay on this wild and beautiful coast – and there are campsites galore as well as the usual holiday accommodation – families have plenty of amusements in the resort towns. Scarborough is the biggest of the seaside attractions, although Filey, Bridlington and Whitby have their share of beach, amusement arcades and other organised entertainment. Whitby's harbour, still a major fishing port despite the loss of the herring trade, is worth many hours' sightseeing. Climb the interminable steps to the 13th-century Abbey (with origins in the 7th-century) see Captain Cook's house in Grape Lane and do not miss out on the kippers sold by Willie Fortune from his shop high above the harbour.

Yorkshire's only salmon river, the Esk runs through a narrow cleft of the moors in beautiful surroundings. There are boats for hire on the river at Sleights and idyllic picnic spots further up the dale at places like Glaisdale. Within easy reach of all the resorts on this coast is the moors centre of Pickering, the

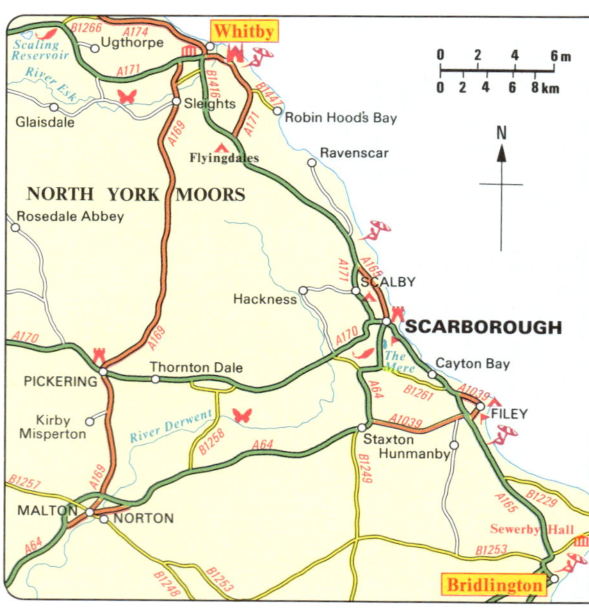

River Derwent (upper reaches)
Fly fishing for trout, plus grayling
Daily tickets: A Pritchard, Eastborough, Scarborough
Tel: (0723) 74017
Water Authority: YWA
Tel: (0532) 448201

River Esk
Offering salmon (a rarity in this county), brown trout & grayling
Daily tickets (in advance): R W Swaby, Millbeck, Ruswarp, Whitby
Tel: (0947) 4658
Tackle shop: E Wilson, 65 Haggersgate, Whitby
Tel: (0947) 3855
Water Authority: as River Derwent

Scaling Reservoir
Trout reservoir near Whitby
Daily tickets: on-site ticket office
Water Authority: YWA

Scarborough Mere
Coarse fishing lake
Daily tickets: on bank
Water Authority: as River Derwent

A fine catch!

Camping
Filey: North Cliff Touring Caravan Site ►►►
Tel: (0723) 66212
Level 122-pitch site
Open Apr–Sep, must book
Fylingdales: Grouse Hill Caravan Park ►►►
Tel: (0947) 880543
Scenic 300-pitch site
Open Apr–Oct, must book Jul–Aug
Scarborough: Scalby Manor Caravan & Camping Site ►►►►
Tel: (0723) 66212
Level 345-pitch site (75 tents)
Open Apr–Oct, must book Jul–Aug

Golfing
Filey:
Tel: (0723) 3293
Windy parkland course, 18 holes, 6020yds, par 70, SSS69
Flamborough Head:
Tel: (0262) 850333
Undulating links course, 18 holes, 5404yds, par 66, SSS66
Scarborough North Cliff:
Tel: (0723) 60786
Seaside course with good views, 18 holes, 6284yds, par 70, SSS70
Whitby:
Tel: (0947) 2768
Breezy links course, 18 holes, 5980yds, par 69, SSS67

Walking Trails
Crow Wood Trail: ¾m (½hr) signposted woodland walk. Start from Danby Lodge Car Park, Danby

General
Bridlington: Sewerby Hall, Park & Zoo: Georgian house in walled garden, with aviary plus miniature zoo
Open all year 9–dusk
Tel: (0262) 73769
Scarborough: Scarborough Castle: 12th-century stronghold
Open all year
Scarborough Zoo & Marineland: bears, monkeys, dolphins, etc
Open Easter–Oct 10–dusk
Tel: (0723) 64401
Whitby: Whitby Abbey: extensive remains of 13th-century church
Open all year
Whitby Museum: specialising in local history, with Pannett Art Gallery next door
Open May–Sep daily 9.30–5.30 (Sun 2–5)
Tel: (0947) 2908

terminus of an eighteen-mile steam railway which chugs through a glacial valley which has no road access.

Just south of Pickering is Kirby Misperton, where Flamingoland is home to over 1 000 animals, birds and reptiles in a 350-acre pleasure park. Nearer to the resort centre is Scarborough's own zoo and marineland where children are given free fish to feed the sealions, dolphins exercise their superior intelligence and penguins play the clown.

For walkers with a stout heart there is the major section of the way-marked Cleveland Way, running for the most part along the cliff tops from Filey, north to Saltburn. This ninety-three-mile path eventually cuts back across the moors to Osmotherly at the National Park's western edge. The twenty-four-hour endurance test of the Lyke Wake Walk follows the Cleveland Way, too, in its traverse across the park to the cliff-top village of Ravenscar. For the less energetic there are short nature trails at Ravenscar, Wykeham, Dalby and Langdale, all offering beautiful scenery.

Despite the presence of a nearby holiday camp, Filey is the least brash of the resorts on this coast. A fishing centre, it also has a scenic parkland golf course and a beach where it is usually possible to escape and be apart from the madding crowds.

Cunning anglers will plan their visit to this stimulating area for late September, when the annual Scarborough Angling Festival is on – nine days of competitive shore and boat matches that provide a feast of fish.

Northumberland Coast

Berwick-upon-Tweed – Tynemouth

Angling Associations
Clubs on the Northumberland coast are affiliated to the Northern Federation of Sea Angling Societies: for information contact: The Secretary, 8 Gainsborough Square, Grindon, Sunderland

Tackle Dealers
Bagnall & Kirkwood, 52 Grey Street, Newcastle
Chartamac, 1A Avenue Terrace, Seaton Delaval
Grey's of Alnwick, 24 Hipsburn Crescent, Lesbury
Rod & Line, High Street, Newbiggin-by-the-Sea
W Temple, 43 Ocean View, Whitley Bay

HM Coastguard
Amble: *Tel: (0665) 710318*
Berwick: *Tel: (0289) 6005*
Newbiggin: *Tel: (067 085) 231*
Seahouses (Rescue HQ): *Tel: (0665) 720274*
Tynemouth: *Tel: (089 45) 72691*

Inland Fishing Water Authority
Northumbrian Water Authority
Tel: Gosforth (0632) 843151

The Northumberland coast shows a vastly changing face to the cold waters of the North Sea. In places, miles of deserted sand are flanked by dunes and peppered with rocky outcrops, while elsewhere the surf breaks on steeply-shelving beaches black with coal dust. Rugged cliffs are veined with gullies and pock-marked with coves; there are estuaries, harbours and the inevitable outcrops of man – piers, breakwaters and jetties. It still holds true that many rock and beach marks have still to be explored and that the piers and jetties never become too crowded.

Codling is the chief target which can be caught throughout the year, despite a main season from early September to January and February. As a rule, sport is best during the winter when the cod shoals move close in and the rough seas unlock the sea bed larder. Dab, whiting, plaice and flounder are a consistent catch depending on seasonal and regional differences, for as the coastline changes with each bay, what is good for one mark is not necessarily right for another.

Sound preparation is the keynote to successful sea angling off this coast. The fisherman who does not mind spending time studying rock marks at low water reaps a rich reward, and strong tackle is essential. Rough seas and rocky bottoms can prove a very costly proposition otherwise.

Obtaining bait is no problem in the north east. Peeler, soft crabs and mussels can be found in many areas and a plethora of tackle shops supply live lug and ragworm (although it should be ordered in advance before setting out on an expedition).

Boat fishing has still not reached the same level of popularity that it enjoys further south, but a few skippers who do take out parties of enthusiasts find it lucrative. The only other way to deeper waters is to hire a dinghy, but this can be folly for the inexperienced as the treachery of the sea in a squall should never be underestimated.

Tynemouth and its wide estuary has first-class beach and rock angling for whatever the weather, some sport can be had from its piers, jetties, beaches, rock marks or the estuary itself. Again, codling is favourite, with coalfish, pouting, dab, plaice, eel and some whiting and mackerel. Cullercoats, just to the north, with its picturesque harbour, has good marks off two breakwaters and outlying reefs, but heavy tackle is needed and one eye should always be kept on the sea, as retreat has to be rapid once the tide rises.

The broad beaches and rocky outcrops of Whitley Bay offer more relaxed, but still satisfying sport, while Seaton Sluice produces its richest harvest from November to March with exciting cod fishing from its cliff edges.

Flatfish and some sizeable cod are taken after a good wintry blow at the industrial port of Blyth, where the River Wansbeck flows out to the sea. Every so often a lucky angler will bag a sea trout instead of the flatties he is after, but anyone setting out to repeat this should first obtain a Northumbria Water Authority licence.

Between Blyth and Alnmouth (another estuary town) the coast is illuminated into the early hours by a thousand lights, as for many, night fishing is the mainstay of the sport. Simple bottom tackle should be used over the rock marks with a weak ledger link to save valuable tide time when they inevitably get snagged. Flounders abound in the sands of the Aln estuary at Alnmouth, with shoals of codling appearing from November onwards. In winter storms one of the best spots for cod is Cullernose Point which surrenders the best only in these inclement conditions – in calmer weather flatfish such as plaice and flounder are good sport and they occur in large quantities.

Rough weather at Craster also yields fine catches of cod, but even without a run of luck the visitor need not go home empty-handed. Craster is famous for its kippers which are oak-smoked in this picture-postcard village.

Bamburgh Castle

At Seahouses, to the south of Bamburgh, a breakwater protects the harbour and gives the holiday angler a chance of catching mackerel and flounders. There is more scope from a boat over deep water marks off the Farne Islands, with a good chance of tangling with large cod, haddock and conger.

Lindisfarne Priory on Holy Island is considered the cradle of Christianity in the north, but it is not only day trippers who negotiate the causeway from the mainland. Shallow sandy bays fish well for flatfish and stretches of deeper water yield larger species found elsewhere only in the autumn. A good supply of bait can be dug at low tide.

Another lovely setting is south of Berwick-upon-Tweed, England's northernmost town, where the coast has been designated an area of Outstanding Natural Beauty. Although justly proud of a reputation for miles of top-class salmon and trout fishing, Berwick has a modest claim to good shore fishing.

Visitors can hardly miss the Tweed. The approach to the town is dominated by three famous bridges, the Old (or Berwick) with fifteen arches, the Royal Tweed roadbridge and the Royal Border bridge of 1850 which carries the railway. Elizabethan walls (said to be the earliest of their period in Europe) and ten feet thick in places, are witness to the town's warlike history. Berwick was the rope in a tug-of-war between the Scots and English and changed hands thirteen times.

Camping
Bamburgh: Beadnell Links ►►►
Tel: (066 589) 241
Level 10-pitch farmland site (no tents)
Open Apr–Oct, must book Jul–Aug
Glororum Caravan Park ►►
Tel: (066 84) 205
Pleasant 100-pitch site (no tents)
Open Apr–Oct, must book Jul–Aug
Belford: Waren Caravan Site ►►►
Tel: (066 84) 366
105-pitch seaside site (15 tents)
Open May–Oct, no bookings

Golfing
Bamburgh Castle:
Tel: (066 84) 378
Short scenic course, 18 holes, 5495yds, par 68, SSS67
Berwick-upon-Tweed (Goswick):
Tel: (0289) 87256
Easy walking links course, 18 holes, 6437yds, par 72, SSS71
Tynemouth:
Tel: (089 45) 74578
Well-drained downland course, 18 holes, 6283yds, par 70, SSS70

Walking Trails
St Mary's Island
Nature Trail: 1¼m (2½hr) signposted, circular walk passing many aviaries. Start 2m N of Whitley Bay seafront off A193

General
Bamburgh:
Bamburgh Castle: imposing Norman fortress
Open Apr–Sep afternoons only. For party tours
Tel: (066 84) 208
Grace Darling Museum: documents & relics of the 19th-century heroine
Open Apr–Sep daily 11–7
Berwick-upon-Tweed: Museum of the King's Own Scottish Borderers: good collection housed in Britain's oldest barracks
Open all year (ex Sat afternoons & Sun)
Tel: (0289) 7426/7
Lindisfarne (or Holy Island): Lindisfarne Priory: very early Christian church accessible only at low tide
Tel: (0289) 87200
Warkworth:
Warkworth Castle: 11th–14th-century stronghold with rare bridge tower
Open Apr–Sep

A respect of the sea is further engendered at the Grace Darling Museum at Bamburgh. In the late 1830's, she and her father (who was keeper of Longstone Lighthouse) rowed out to save five people from a wrecked steamboat, the *Forfarshire*. To the north west lies almost land-locked Budle Bay, the haunt of many wild birds. Boat trips are available to Farne Islands, once the home of St Aidan and St Cuthbert, and the breeding ground for many species of interesting sea birds.

Shakespeare was so impressed by the remains of the 12th-century castle at Warkworth that he used it to set the scene in part of his Henry IV. A hermitage chapel cut out of solid rock can be reached by rowing boat from the castle and there is a sandy beach for sunbathing.

On a cloudy day, visit Seaton Delaval Hall, a Baroque-style, 18th-century masterpiece of Vanbrugh, where one exquisite wing was built to house the stables, but book in advance for the Hall's 'mediaeval' banquets.

South are the attractions of Tynemouth, a resort on the north banks of the Tyne. The 11th-century Priory and later castle are only ruins but make a good viewpoint out to sea. An inlet known as Priors Haven is popular for bathing, sunbathing and, for children of all ages, building sandcastles.

The wild and beautiful coastline of Northumberland is still one of England's best-kept secrets, where miles of beach and countryside remain untouched by the feet of tourists each year. Sea anglers will enjoy the pioneer spirit of finding for themselves a rich hunting ground from a rock or jetty and non-enthusiasts can sight-see, relax on deserted beaches or enjoy the invigorating air from the clifftops over-looking the windswept sea.

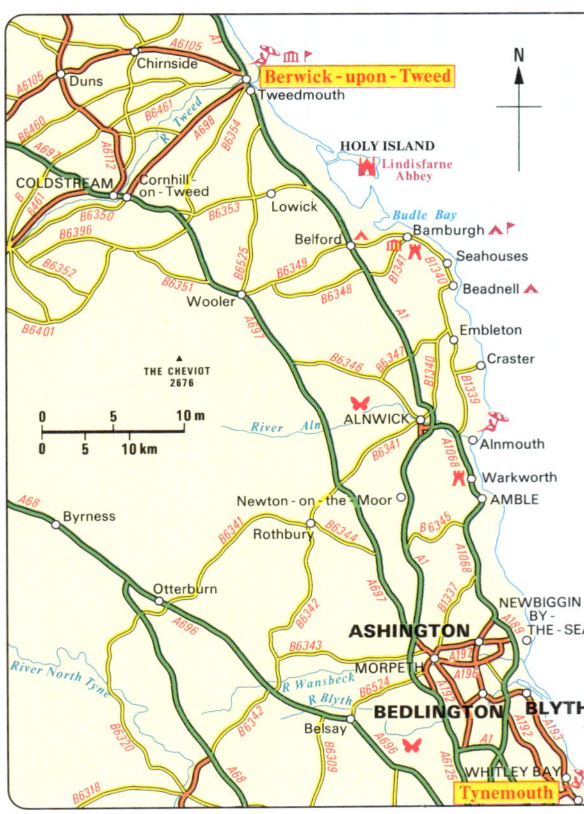

River Aln
Salmon plus fly fishing for trout
Daily tickets (in advance): Hardy Bros, Willowburn Trading Estate, Alnwick
Tel: (0665) 2771
Water Authority: NWA
Tel: (0632) 843151

Alnmouth
Good sea fishing for cod, flatfish and mackerel plus the trout

Berwick
Good rock fishing at Bears Head for cod and flatfish, whilst boat fishing may yield numerous whiting

River Blyth
Trout plus grayling and roach, but still recovering from effects of pollution
Daily tickets: Bedlington & Blagdon Angling Club (S Symons), 8 Moorland Drive, Bedlington
Tel: (0670) 822011
Water Authority: as River Aln

Blyth
Coalfish, codling, eel, dab, flounder and plaice from the staithes upriver to beyond the ferry. The exposed West Pier fishes well for codling, dab, eel, flounder, gurnard, plaice and whiting. Codling, coalfish and flatfish may be fished from the beach

Angler's Directory for the North of England

Clubs and Associations

Aln Angling Association (F J R Moir), Thistledowne, 49 Swansfield Park Road, Alnwick, Northumberland
Tel: (0665) 602565
Bedlington and Blagdon Angling Club (S Symons), 8 Moorland Drive, Bedlington, Northumberland
Tel: (0670) 822011
Berwick and District Angling Club (A R Manderson), 56 Westfield Road, Berwick-upon-Tweed, Northumberland
Boroughbridge and District Angling Association (J Coates), Jasmine Cottage, New Row, Boroughbridge, North Yorkshire
Bradford City Angling Association (A Scaife), 80 Whetley Hill, Bradford 8, West Yorkshire
Tel: (0274) 47799
Bridlington Angling Association (W Farr), 53 Milner Road, Bridlington, Humberside
Calder Angling Association (W N Nixon), 1 Yottenfews, Calderbridge, Seascale, Cumbria
Coniston and Torver Angling Association (N Dixon), 2 Lake View, Coniston, Cumbria
Egremont Angling Association (C Fisher), 69 North Road, Egremont, Cumbria
Filey Brigg Angling Society (M Lavington), 34 Scarborough Road, Filey, North Yorkshire
Tel: (0723) 512026
Gosforth Angling Association, Holmelea, Gosforth, Seascale, Cumbria
Kent (Cumbria) Angling Association (J C Parkin), 11a Blea Tarn Road, Kendal, Cumbria
Keswick Angling Association (H Collinson), 16 Latrigg Close, Keswick, Cumbria
Knaresborough Piscatorial Society (G Binks), 14 St Andrew Place, Harrogate, North Yorkshire
Leeds and District Amalgamated Society of Anglers, Anglers Club, Stoney Rock Lane, Beckett Street, Leeds, West Yorkshire
Northern Angling Association (G Wilson), 11 Guildford Avenue, Chorley, Lancashire
Tel: (025 72) 65905
Penrith Angling Association (R F Allinson), 7 Scaws Drive, Penrith, Cumbria
Ripon Angling Club (A R Trees), Borrage Lane, Ripon, North Yorkshire
Tel: (0765) 3143
Ripon Piscatorial Society (P Godden), 3 Oak Road, Ripon, North Yorkshire
Scarborough Boat Angling Club (J A Martin), 26 Ling Hill, Newby, Scarborough, North Yorkshire
Tel: (0723) 75590
Scarborough Rock Angling Club (H Dobson), 1 Uplands Avenue, East Ayton, Scarborough, North Yorkshire
Thornaby Angling Association (A G Butler), 5 Nelsonby Grove, Hartburn, Stockton-on-Tees, Cleveland
Wensleydale Angling Association (T Fawcett), 12 The Crescent, Bainbridge, North Yorkshire.
Windermere, Ambleside and District Angling Association (R Parry), Yew Bank, Clappersgate, Ambleside, Cumbria

Tackle Shops

Alnwick
Alnwick Sports Centre, Narrowgate
Tel: (0665) 602462
Bowness
P Musgrave & Son, Lake Road
Tel: (096 62) 2133
Bridlington
H Buckley, Harbour Road
Linford's Fishing Tackle, 12 Hilderthorpe Road
Tel: (0262) 78045
Filey
Dale's, 12 Hope Street
Tel: (0723) 512123
Kendal
E Atkinson, Strickland Gate
Tel: (0539) 20300
Leyburn
F Reek, High Street
Wray Bros, Town Hall
Tel: (0969) 22150
Ripon
R C Hodgson, 7 Queen Street
Tel: (0765) 3029
B Wain, 82 Bondgate
Scarborough
H Buckley, Anglers' Supplies, Leading Post Street
Tel: (0723) 63202
A Pritchard, 56 Eastborough
Tel: (0723) 74017
P & B Somers (boat hire)
Tel: (0723) 890143
Whitby
R Blackburn, 6 South Terrace
Tel: (0947) 2478
J Grayson (boat hire), 42 Brook Park, Sleights
Tel: (0947) 81606
E Wilson, 65 Haggersgate
Tel: (0947) 3855
Whitley Bay
W Temple, 43 Ocean View Drive
Tel: (0632) 526017
Windermere
See Bowness

Water Authorities

Northumbrian Water Authority, Northumbria House, Regent Centre, Gosforth, Newcastle-upon-Tyne, Tyne and Wear
Tel: (0632) 843151
North West Water Authority, New Town House, Buttermarket Street, Warrington, Cheshire
Tel: (0925) 53999
Yorkshire Water Authority, West Riding House, 67 Albion Street, Leeds, West Yorkshire
Tel: (0532) 448201

Hotels and Inns

Alnmouth
Schooner Hotel
Tel: (066 573) 216
Alnwick
Alnwick Hotel
White Swan
Tel: (0665) 602109
Ambleside
Salutation Hotel
Tel: (096 63) 2244
Berwick-upon-Tweed
King's Arms
Tel: (0289) 7454
Boroughbridge
Black Lion
Tel: (090 12) 2253
Filey
Hylands Hotel
Tel: (0723) 512091
White Lodge
Tel: (0723) 512268
Kendal
Globe Inn
Tel: (0539) 24042
The Woolpack
Tel: (0539) 23852
Ripon
Studley Royal Hotel
Tel: (0765) 2044
Unicorn Hotel
Tel: (0765) 2202
Scarborough
Everley Hotel, Hackness
Tel: (0723) 82202
Windermere
Old England Hotel
Tel: (096 62) 2444
Windermere Hotel
Tel: (096 62) 2251

5

South Scotland

Solway Firth

Portpatrick – Gretna

Angling Associations
Dalbeattie and District Sea Angling Club
Kirkcudbright Sea Angling Club
Mull of Galloway Big Game Club

Tackle Dealers
The Flotsam, Harbour Road, Isle of Whithorn
Kippford Slipway Ltd, Kippford, Dalbeattie
W McKinnell, 15 Cuthbert Street, Kirkcudbright
Morton Nash, Tonderghie Road, Isle of Whithorn
The Sports Shop, George Street, Stranraer

HM Coastguard
(no fully manned stations on Scottish coast of Solway Firth)
Greenock: *Tel: (0475) 29014*
Isle of Man: *Tel: (0624) 813255*

Inland fishing
No controlled waters in Dumfries and Galloway area – seek permission of riparian owner or holder of fishing rights

A coastline punctuated by headlands and offshore reefs, lapped by stray, warm currents from the Gulf Stream and torn by strong tidal runs, the Solway Firth is one of Scotland's prime sea angling areas. Realisation of its potential has only come in recent years.

The Solway is a treasure-trove for tope, with fish weighing-in at the 50lb mark, and superb sport for lunker halibut and skate. The Mull of Galloway has so far produced two records – a 19lb thornback ray and a 15½lb bull huss, both taken from the shore. On the Kirkcudbrightshire coast, shore marks regularly produce large cod in winter months.

The rivers that drain into the Solway are also comparatively unexploited. Many lower stretches of the border river Esk yield good dace, chub and grayling, although the river is better known for a large annual run of sea trout. There is a similar choice of fish from the Annan, where a 10lb chub broke the then-record some years ago – and stretches of this river can be fished on Sundays. Perhaps even less known and under-exploited are the rivers further west. The ill-fated Nith, recovering from a history of set-backs, promises to be a first-class salmon river one day; the River Dee with pike fishing at its source in Loch Ken; and the Urr, sandwiched between the two, a summer and late autumn salmon river. Also of note are the trout and salmon rivers of Fleet, Cree and Luce.

As a rule of thumb, the best sea angling sport in the Solway is to be had at the west end around the Mull of Galloway, Luce Bay and the Isle of Whithorn. Larger species diminish eastwards towards Gretna. Portpatrick, a small holiday resort and fishing village on the west coast of Wigtownshire has good shore fishing from many rocky points, with Yellow Isle (half a mile north of the harbour), Sandeel Bay and Killintringan Lighthouse among the best. A day's catch could include a wide variety of species – pollack, coalfish, plaice, flounder, codling, mackerel, dogfish, conger, wrasse and the occasional tope. One drawback is that bait is not sold locally, so a detour to a Stranraer tackle shop has to be made, or you make an early start to dig lugworm east of the town's railway pier.

Several charter boats, among them Bryn Watson's *Appache*, take anglers to deeper waters, where rewards are large tope, common skate, thornback and good dab and plaice. Conger up to 20lb can be taken on fish baits and mackerel are usually plentiful throughout the area.

Port Logan, to the south, is one of the few places where the angler can launch his own boat, particularly if easterly winds prevent sport in Luce Bay. However it is essential that local advice is sought beforehand, as the tides around the Mull are ferocious, and boats incapable of at least ten knots are not recommended in these waters.

Drummore is the main port for anglers wishing to fish the western side of Luce Bay. A plethora of hotels and guest houses receive an end-of-season bonus from visitors after big autumn tope which can run to more than 50lb, and the occasional porbeagle shark. Between here and Port William are miles of sandy beaches and white breaker lines with warm waters that teem with bass, flatfish, plaice, flounder and dab. At Sandhead there is more bass on a flood tide, especially at night during summer and early autumn.

The tidal harbour and hire boats of Port William await those set on fishing the lower waters of Luce Bay, where tope are the common prize from mid-June to October. There are good shore marks, too, at Monreith Bay, still enjoying a reputation as a good bass beach, especially on night tides. A picturesque harbour at Isle of Whithorn sees as many amateur sailors as anglers in summer months and so information on sea and weather conditions is

Portpatrick harbour

willingly given by the coastguard station in the village. Boat fishermen can expect catches of ray, bull huss and the prolific tope, or shark in the tidal races at Burrow Head. There is less exhilarating sport in the sheltered waters of Wigtown Bay (cod, conger, ray, mackerel, spurdog), and fishing from the rocks (pollack, wrasse, eel and bass). Plenty of rag and lugworm are available locally.

Kirkcudbright's rugged coastline deters small boat fishermen, although there is good general fishing over three miles out to sea. Casting from the shore is equally varied, with landbass, coalfish, cod and pollack from marks at the tidal harbour and wooden jetty.

Cod abound in the Solway throughout the year and the Scottish shore record (37lb) came from Rockcliffe during the winter run. Although cod stocks are reputed to be depleted compared to a few years ago, specimens of over 30lb are taken each winter. Other good shore marks for cod are to be found from Balcary Point to Kippford.

This area enjoys particularly temperate, un-Scottish weather and luxuriant, sub-tropical gardens, open to the public are nearby at Arbigland, Kirkbean, at Kinmount and Ruthwell with Castle Kennedy, Ardwell and Port Logan further west. All are at their best between April and September. Semi-precious stones and minerals from all over the world are displayed at Creetown's museum and art gallery, together with a collection of walking sticks and drinking mugs.

Dumfries and Galloway is rich in abbeys, gracious stately homes and historic houses, Rammerscales, an elegant Georgian mansion at Lochmaben, has links with the Russian Tzars, and Sweetheart Abbey, New Abbey, remains a beautiful shell of an abbey founded by Lady Devorgilla in memory of her husband John Balliol. Dundrennan Abbey is an interesting 12th-century Cistercian relic.

Several ruined castles dot the countryside – a reminder of fierce and bloody Border feuds. The Maxwell clan was thoroughly thrashed at Lockerbie and its great triangular fortress at Caerlaverock Castle was once the family's chief seat. There is a nature reserve near the ruins, among the salt marshes and sandy foreshore of the Nith Estuary, which is noted for its wildfowl (including rare barnacle geese), especially in winter.

Scotland's celebrated poet Robert Burns spent much of his time around here and died at Dumfries after taking a 'health cure' in the icy waters of the Solway at Brow Well. His house is now a museum of his effects and nearby in St Michael's churchyard is a mausoleum in memoriam. Parts of the Burns Heritage Trail which follow the Solway shore are well sign-posted and lace through some of the most enchanting countryside in the county. (Details of the Trail are obtainable from the Scottish Tourist Board in Edinburgh.)

One reason why the Dee declined as a fishing river was because a hydro-electricity plant was built in the estuary at Tongland. The family can visit the dam and power station (a bus collects visitors from Kirkcudbright), while keen anglers travel upstream to try their luck. It is not unusual for interests to coincide in this way. This part of Scotland is steeped in beauty and history, veined by rivers and the cod and tope-rich waters of the Solway are edged by miles of sandy beaches which are guaranteed to occupy any angler's family.

Camping
Annan: Queensberry Bay Caravan Park ►►►
Tel: (046 17) 205
Quiet 25-pitch site
Open Apr–Oct, must book Jul–Aug
Glenluce: Cock Inn Caravan Park ►►►
Tel: (058 15) 227
Partly sloping 75-pitch site (5 tents), 5m SE of Glenluce
Open Mar–Oct, must book Jul–Aug
Gretna: Braids Caravan Site ►
Tel: (046 13) 409
Peaceful 30-pitch site
Open Apr–Oct, must book Jul–Aug

Golfing
Portpatrick:
Tel: (0776) 81273
Links course with natural hazards, 18 holes, 5505yds, par 70, SSS67
Powfoot (Annan):
Tel: (046 17) 227
Delightful seaside course, 18 holes, 6283yds, par 71, SSS70

General
Annan: Kinmount Gardens: extensive gardens including woodland trails & picnic areas
Open Apr–Oct daily 9–5
Caerlaverock: Caerlaverock Castle: noted mediaeval fortress 9m S of Dumfries off B725
Open all year
Wildfowl Trust: fine views, plus numerous bird flocks
Open Sep–mid-May tours at 11 & 2 daily
Tel: (038 777) 200
Dundrennan: Dundrennan Abbey: remains of 12th-century Cistercian house
Open all year
Port Logan: Logan Botanic Garden: containing comprehensive range of plants & shrubs
Open Apr–Sep daily 10–5
Tel: (077 686) 231
Whithorn: Whithorn Priory: ruins of first Christian church in Scotland, plus museum housing rare MSS
Open all year

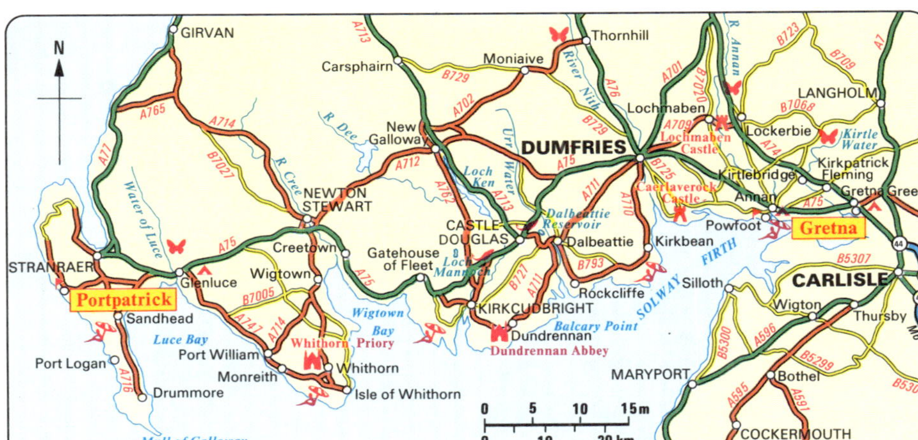

River Annan
Good sea trout in upper reaches during summer, with fair chances for the visitor
Daily tickets (keeper): T Nelson, Newbie Mill, Annan
Tel: (046 12) 2292

Dalbeattie Reservoir
Regularly re-stocked stillwater offering good rainbow trout
Daily tickets (from café): N Parker, 30 High Street, Dalbeattie

Kirtle Water
Mainly trout, best in late summer
Free fishing at Kirtlebridge

Lairdmannoch Loch
Fly fishing for trout, from boats only
Daily tickets (riparian owner): Lidderdale & Gillespie Ltd, National Bank Building, Castle Douglas
Tel: (0556) 2314

Water of Luce
Mixed fishing from bay to Glenluce
Daily tickets: Stranraer & District Angling Association (J D Kinross), Balnacoil, Larg Road, Stranraer
Tel: (0776) 3312

River Nith
Fine salmon fishing, with good opportunities for non-residents
Daily tickets: D McMillan, 6 Friars Vennel, Dumfries
Tel: (0387) 2075

River Tweed

Angling Associations
County of Peebles Angling Improvement Association
Gala Angling Club
Hawick Angling Club
Melrose and District Angling Association
Peeblesshire Salmon Fishing Association

Tackle dealers and other ticket sources
Buccleugh Estate, Estates Office, Eckford
Crainey Tackle Shop, High Street, Innerleithen
Dryburgh Abbey Hotel, St Boswells
Ednam House Hotel, Kelso
Ian Fraser's Sports Centre, Northgate, Peebles
George and Abbotsford Hotel, Melrose
The Luckenbooth, High Street, Innerleithen
Peebles Town Council, Peebles
Redpath & Co, Horse Market, Kelso
Rod & Gun, St John's Street, Galashiels
Tweed Valley Hotel, Walkerburn
W R Wells, 17 Northgate, Peebles

Close Seasons
Salmon: December 1 – January 31, *trout:* October 7 – March 14 (some local variations, notably County of Peebles AIA Water October 1 – March 30), *coarse fish:* no closed season in Scotland (note, on some waters all coarse fish caught must be killed)

Rising in the hills of Tweedsmuir, only three miles or so from the fount of the Clyde, the hundred-mile Tweed is a very Scottish river – only in its last fifteen miles does it form the northern border of Northumberland and England. Once thought to be the premier game river of the British Isles, it is a title the Tweed has had to relinquish to the Tay over the last fifty years. It is second only to the Tay in one other aspect – the tremendous area of its watershed. In this 1 900 square miles of hillside and forest, hundreds of burns and some major river tributaries swell the Tweed, giving rise to superb pools among the hundreds of beats renowned for producing salmon from 8lb in the spring to 24lb in the autumn.

Not the least of the Tweed's many charms is that it is without a doubt the most accessible of the major game rivers to the visiting angler. It is far from cheap – in the 1980 season a day's salmon fishing will cost between £5 and £40, but trout fishing and the many coarse fishing opportunities of the lower waters are on a par with other less-favoured waters. Visitors should also bear in mind a complex set of regulations covering the types of fishing allowed in certain areas and the variation in close seasons operated on some reaches.

The principal rules are that to fish for trout, an angler must have written permission before setting foot on the bank, so obtain your day ticket in advance. The salmon season is generally from February 1st to November 30th, but for a long section of the upper water from Peebles down to Scrogbank, below Walkerburn, the season opens on February 21st. An age-old, and rather illogical link between rod-and-line rules and the netting season means that the Tweed is for fly-fishing only from February 1st–14th and from September 5th to November 30th. In common with most Scottish waters, Sunday fishing of any kind is severely limited.

For salmon fishing, most visitor's chances fall in the waters above the Tweed-Teviot junction at Kelso, as the very productive lower waters through Coldstream to Berwick are very tightly tied up. It is worth mentioning the 600-yard left bank beat from Leet Water to the road bridge at Coldstream (day tickets from the bailiff), waters available from the Tillmouth Park Hotel, Cornhill-on-Tweed, Coldstream (available to residents and occasionally offered to personal applicants on the day), and the trout and coarse permits available from the Masons Arms, Norham. Also the Milne–Graden beat of the lower river is controlled by Houndwood House at Reston with fine sea trout coming up-river in July and August and the bigger salmon running mainly in September and October.

Around Kelso some waters on the Tweed and the Teviot are controlled by the Kelso Association who issue day tickets. Two opportunities to sample the waters of the Teviot, a fine river for spring salmon fishing well from February to April and having a healthy stock of brown trout, are the Hawick Angling Club waters and those of the Buccleugh Estate.

The St Boswells, Melrose and Galashiels area of the river has few opportunities for visitors unless you are a hotel resident. The George and Abbotsford Hotel, Melrose, The Dryburgh Abbey Hotel, St Boswells and the self-catering Ogilvie Dickson Holiday Homes, Galashiels are places to head for. This is, however, a reach of the river noted for trout and grayling with plenty of opportunities to try for them; Melrose and District Angling Association and J and A Turnbull in Galashiels both issue tickets.

Quite the best salmon fishing access of all is on the ten-mile Peeblesshire Salmon Fishing Association Water which stretches from Wyre Bridge Pool (one mile below Peebles town) to Scrogbank below Walkerburn with only a few private beats intervening. It is a water on which few worthwhile salmon are taken early in the season and the pace hots up only in the summer with the arrival of good sea trout and, from early September, the autumn salmon.

Flies favoured by local rods are tubes such as Garry Dog, Thunder and Lightning, Yellow and Black and Stoat's Tail. A local regulation is that two- and three-fly combinations should have no larger than a size four hook, weighting flies or leaders is not allowed and single hooks are to be no larger than 4/0. From March 15th to September 14th baits and lures are allowed. Silver Sprat, Yellow Belly Devon and Brown and Gold lures are locally favoured and, if you prefer spoons, try Zebra Toby or Mepps types. Early-season fishermen may find they have young kelts on the hook. These must be handled carefully and returned to the water live.

Trout fishing can be superb in this area and some of the best opportunities are held by the County of Peebles Angling Improvement Association with nearly thirty miles of water on the Tweed and tributaries above Peebles town (where the local council hold the rights). It was for the Tweed's trout that Canon Greenwell invented Greenwell's Glory, emulating a medium olive fly. While the best trout are taken in April and May, a summer evening's fishing can result in a good bag. For good fun, especially for youngsters and beginners, the Association's beats on Lyne Water above Peebles offers trout up to the 1lb mark and some big grayling. This small stream has very good, accessible banks.

If you are not fortunate enough to be staying in a fishing hotel or in the choice of self-catering units in the area, there are a string of campsites close to the water from Peebles to Kelso. Most of them will help with fishing arrangements.

The course of the Tweed through the countryside of Peebles and the Borders is a land of Sir Walter Scott, John Buchan and the sturdy woollen fabrics which bear the river's name. Probably called 'tweed' by a happy corruption of the Scots dialect *tweel* (or twill), the cloth is made from sheep grazing the Cheviots. The industry is commemorated at the Museum of Wool Textiles in Walkerburn with its working exhibits of hand spinning and weaving. More modern fabric design and production can be seen at the Bernat Klein Exhibition, Waukrigg Mill, in Galashiels, where the designer's notes

Camping
Hawick: Riverside Caravan Park ►►►
Tel: (0450) 3785
Level 50-pitch site
Open Apr–Oct, no bookings
Kelso: Springwood Caravan Park ►►►
Tel: (057 32) 2596
Secluded 30-pitch site (no tents)
Open Apr–Sep, must book Jul–Aug
Melrose: Gibson Park Caravan Site ►►
Tel: (0896) 4751 ext 47
Quiet, sloping 50-pitch site (20 caravans)
Open Apr–Sep, must book

Golfing
Galashiels:
Tel: (0896) 3724
Scenic hillside course, 18 holes, 5500yds, par 69, SSS67
Hawick:
Tel: (0450) 2293
Breezy hillside course, 18 holes, 5980yds, par 68, SSS69

Walking Trails
Dundock Wood: various nature trails within large shrubby grounds 1½m W of Coldstream off A697

General
Duns: Jim Clark Room: all trophies won by the motor-racing ace
Open Apr–Sep (Sun afternoons only)
Gordon: Mellerstain House: 18th-century house, plus terraced gardens & lake
Jedburgh: Castle Jail: ex-county prison on site of mediaeval castle, with museum
Open Apr–Sep 10–5 (Sun 1–5)
Tel: (0450) 3457
Manderston: fine Edwardian house with extensive grounds
Open mid-May–mid-Sep (Sun & Thur) 2–5.30
Tel: (036 12) 3450
Melrose: Melrose Abbey: beautiful ruins of Cistercian abbey
Open all year
Selkirk: Selkirk Museum: interesting local crafts, tools & photograph exhibition
Open Jun–Sep 2–5 (Mon–Fri)
Tel: (0750) 20096

and sketches, the inspiration for his patterns are on display.

The area abounds with stately homes, and the ruins of the famous Border Abbeys built at the behest of David 1st. Traquair House near Innerleithen is thought to be one of the oldest inhabited places in Scotland. Since the 11th-century, this riverside park and mansion has played host to royalty (including Mary Queen of Scots) – one owner even had to divert the Tweed when the river threatened the foundations. Peter Maxwell-Stuart, today's owner, brews a special ale in the manor's restored brewery and sells it as one of the many souvenirs of this uniquely romantic house.

Perhaps one of the more delightful aspects of the Tweed is that the best angling is during the spring, late summer and autumn when few other tourists are in the area.

It is a time when the river and the many other attractions along its banks can be enjoyed at a leisurely pace. It is also, happily, the time when accommodation is most readily available, often at attractive low season rates.

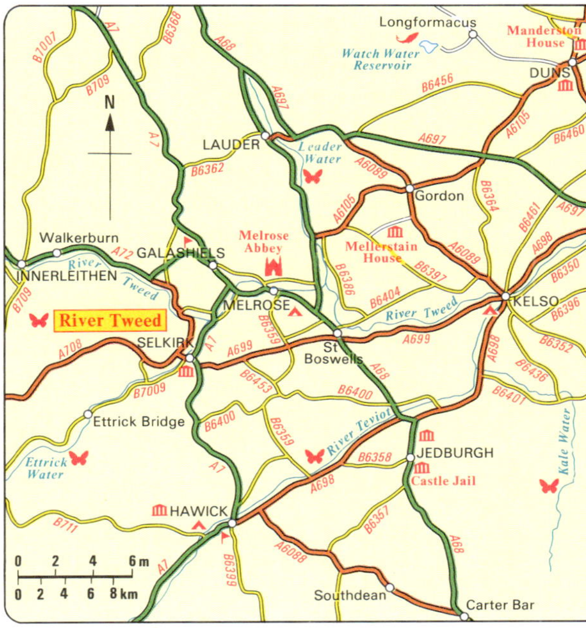

Ettrick Water
Good trout and fair spring salmon run, with some chances for the visitor
Daily tickets: D & H McDonald, 9–11 High Street, Selkirk
Tel: (0750) 21398

Kale Water
A Teviot stream offering trout and some coarse fish
Daily tickets: as River Teviot

Leader Water
Good fishing for smallish trout
Daily tickets (in advance): McQuillan & Wilson, High Street, Earlston, Kelso

River Teviot
Major Tweed tributary offering good trout and grayling
Daily tickets: Keeper's House, Eckford

Watch Reservoir
Fly fishing for trout
Daily tickets: on bank or Rathbourne Hotel, Longformacus, Duns
Tel: (036 17) 232

Salmon fishing near Innerleithen

River Tay

Perth – Pitlochry

Angling Associations
Aberfeldy Angling Club
Perth & District Angling Association
Pitlochry Angling Club

Tackle shops and other ticket sources
Ballathie Estate Office, Ballathie Farms, Stanley, Perth
Director of Finance, Perth and Kinross DC, 1 High Street, Perth
Dunkeld House Hotel, Dunkeld
Grandtully Castle Estate Office, Grandtully, Aberfeldy
Grandtully Hotel, Strathtay
L Jamieson, Sports Shop, Dunkeld Street, Aberfeldy
The Estate Office, Killiechassie, Aberfeldy
Loch Tay Guest House, Kenmore
Logierait Hotel, Ballinluig
P D Malloch (Field Sports) Ltd, 24 Scott Street, Perth
Major Neil Ramsay & Co, Farleyer, Aberfeldy
Renton, Finlayson & Co, 29 Barossa Place, Perth *and at* The Estate Office, Aberfeldy
R Scott Miller, The Tackle Shop, Atholl Street, Dunkeld
Sport in Scotland, 6A High Street, Dunfermline

Close Seasons
Salmon: October 16 – January 14, *trout:* October 7 – March 14 (note: season varies on some stocked stillwaters), *coarse fish:* there is no closed season for coarse fishing in Scotland (note: all roach caught in the Tay must be killed)

If big is supposed to be beautiful, then the River Tay takes all the honours. It is not just the single river; an enormous system of lochs and tributaries make it the biggest water system in Britain by sheer volume. Few would argue that it is Europe's finest river for the consistency of its Atlantic salmon run. Entering the system from the Firth of Tay, through Perth itself and up into the expanses of Lochs Tay and Rannoch and the major tributaries such as the Tummel, Lyon, Garry, Tilt, Isla and Almond, the King of fishes has a vast watershed for a breeding ground. It is an area which is a magnificent mixture of Highland and Lowland Scottish scenery, clean waters against clear and uncluttered horizons. Snowcapped mountains are just visible to the extreme north.

Even for visitors who lack the remotest interest in casting a fly over the Tay, the sight of thousands of these splendid fish making their annual pilgrimage up-river is a stirring sight. You can view them doing just that in the underwater viewing room of the hydro-electric generating station of Faskally near Pitlochry. This fish ladder on the Tummel allows an energetic passage for over 10 000 fish a year from May to early October. The total number of fish in the Tay system can, at best, only be a staggering guess.

Of course, good salmon fishing is becoming increasingly expensive – some stretches could never have been described as cheap. For the visitor, however, there are some chances to get on the water as long as you plan well ahead. The best available beats, on the waters some twenty miles north of Perth upstream, are hotel waters, but there are additional opportunities for the non-resident on the Tay itself and on tributaries.

As the Tay is a heavy-flower (even when apparently at its lowest mark) techniques differ slightly from those on other rivers. Much of the fishing takes place from boats, with up to three rods aboard, fishing from the stern with the ghillie in control. The most popular lure is the Kynoch plug, especially when the water is high, as heavy lures can be supported by the flow. If you prefer spoons, the Toby is widely used in sizes up to 30g or Devon minnows up to 3in can lure the fish in lower water conditions. A tip is to use a metal minnow, as this allows a longer cast and gives the chance of fully covering a salmon lie. Fly fishermen go for larger tubes in the spring, fining down as the season progresses and then going up to 2½in for the autumn. Whatever the type of fishing you pursue, use a 15–20lb line and remember this is a big river – have at least 75 yards of backing on the reel.

The Tay is also a big enough river to allow trout fishermen a slice of the action. It is an almost ideal fly-fishing river, despite the fact that the wading is extremely difficult in places. Breast waders are the rule and be very careful – what appears to be slack water can still have a forceful flow. Greenwell's Glory, the March Brown and the Black Spider hold sway here, although occasional spates of coloured water (generally below the Isla) might require such flies as Peter Ross, Grouse and Green or Woodcock and Yellow.

At Perth the salmon are running fast, straight from the sea, and catches are not large. There is, however, the possibility of fishing the entire water within the city boundaries on a Perth and Kinross District Council ticket available from the council offices (Tourist Office on Saturday). Weekly lets are the rule on the Ballathie Estate beat near Stanley, but there is the occasional day's fishing available. On the Dunkeld House Hotel's beat there is free bank fishing for up to eight residents and occasional unbooked days on the hotel boat. Trout fishing tickets for this area are from The Tackle Shop, Dunkeld.

Ballinluig is the junction of the Tummel and Tay where the Logierait Hotel has several beats available to non-residents. On the Tummel, the Pine Trees Hotel has the north bank for salmon, while the south bank is the preserve of the Pitlochry Angling Club – both have a few opportunities for visitors. The club also controls a five-mile stretch of the Tummel for trout and grayling fishing.

Back on the main river, the best chances for a ticket are afforded by the Grandtully Hotel

A tussle on the Tay near Dunkeld

and Estate Office of Grandtully Castle. The Loch Tay Guest House and Killiechassie Estate Office are two further possibilities in the Aberfeldy area of the river.

If you are unable to book in to any of the beats mentioned above, there are a number of agencies in the area which deal with rods on the Tay. Some chances for single days come late in the booking season (say six months before late season and three months before low season). Try Sport in Scotland, Dunfermline;

Camping
Dunkeld: Erigmore House Caravan Park ►►►►
Tel: (035 02) 236
Flattish 80-pitch site
Open Apr–Oct, no bookings
Inver Mill Caravan Site ►
Grassy 50-pitch site (no tents)
Open Apr–Oct, no bookings
Perth: Cleeve Caravan Park ►►
Tel: (0738) 25662
Level 60-pitch site (no tents)
Open Easter–Oct, no bookings

Golfing
Perth: Craigie Hill:
Tel: (0738) 24377
Undulating parkland course, 18 holes, 5288yds, par 66, SSS66
King James VI:
Tel: (0738) 25170
Parkland course on Tay island, 18 holes, 6037yds, par 70, SSS69
Pitlochry:
Tel: (0796) 2114
Varied heathland course, 18 holes, 5811yds, par 69, SSS68

General
Dunkeld: Loch of Lowes Wild Life Reserve: rare waterfowl, plus indoor exhibition
Open Apr–Sep daily
Tel: (035 02) 337 or *267* off-season
Perth: Black Watch Regimental Museum: numerous items of 42nd/73rd Highland regiment
Open all year
Tel: (0738) 26287 ext 3
Elcho Castle: well-preserved 16th-century fortress 5m SE of Perth
Open all year
Pitlochry: Pitlochry Power Station, Dam & Fish Pass: permanent hydro-electricity exhibition
Open Easter–Oct
Scone: Scone Palace: historic royal & religious centre
Open May–early Oct 10–6 (Sun 2–6)

Renton, Finlayson & Co Perth and Aberfeldy; Major Neil Ramsay & Co, Farleyer; and Malloch (Field Sports) Ltd, Perth.

Key towns for tourists are Perth (and nearby Stanley), Dunkeld, Pitlochry (close to the Tummel/Tay junction) and Aberfeldy. Camping is a good alternative to self-catering, guest house or hotel accommodation. There are excellent sites throughout the region.

Perth is inevitably the tourist magnet of the area. The city commands the mouth of the Tay in an imposing strategic position, which is reflected in the Museum of the formidable Black Watch at Balhousie Castle. This is one of the many houses open to the public within a mile or two of Perth. In a carry-over from the Tweed, Perth, too, has its Walter Scott associations. The Fair Maid's House of the 14th-century was the home of Simon Glover, whose daughter Catherine became the heroine of *Fair Maid of Perth*. Buchan's *Huntingtower* was inspired by Ruthven Castle, now actually called by the novel's name.

Pitlochry not only has the fascinating salmon leap, it is a golfing, rambling and pony-trekking centre. Just outside the town is the Faskally Wayside Centre, which provides picnic facilities on the bank of Loch Faskally, a children's play area and a way-marked nature trail. Only a few miles on, the A9 brings you to the site of the battle of Killiecrankie in which King William's troops were routed by Jacobites under 'Bonnie Dundee' in 1689. The Trust Visitor Centre has a battle display reliving this famous clash of dirk and sword.

High above the middle reaches of the Tay at Dunkeld is the Loch of Lowes, which feeds a tributary of the Isla and thence the Tay. The loch is a wild life reserve, where a variety of waterfowl, including the great crested grebe (once an endangered species), can be seen in natural surroundings from an observation hide equipped with high power binoculars. You could return to Perth from here via Scone Palace, one of the oldest-known seats of Scottish royalty and religion. Scottish kings were crowned here until 1651 and it has been a religious centre for over 1 000 years.

Above all, Tayside is a region of contrast, where Scotland is split in two. From the pastoral scenery of the south, Tayside turns to the rugged majesty of moor and mountain in the north. The Tay itself reflects these contrasts. Fearsome in spate and tranquil in its depths, this huge volume of water slips to the sea calling its rich harvest from the ocean to the hard-fighting end that befits the King of fish.

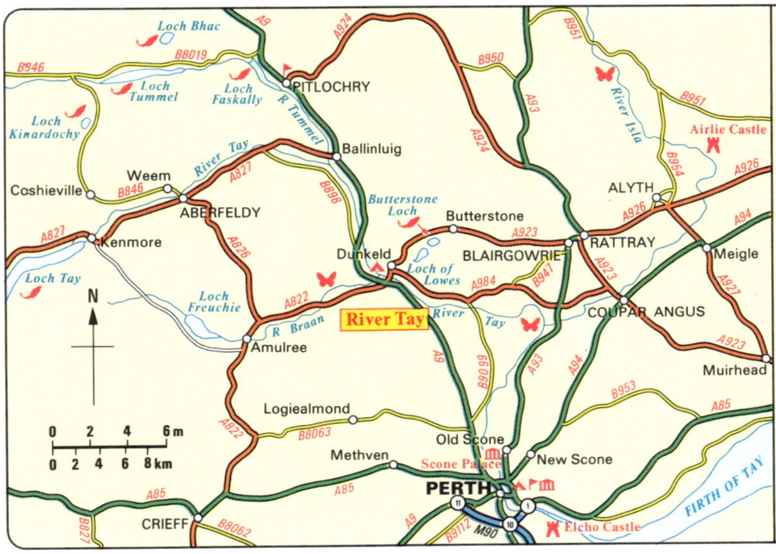

Loch Bhac
Fly fishing from bank for trout near Pitlochry
Daily tickets: Pitlochry Angling Club, c/o Pitlochry Tourist Office, 28 Atholl Road, Pitlochry
Tel: (0796) 2215

River Braan
Trout stream with some chances for visitors
Daily tickets: Amulree Hotel, Amulree
Tel: (035 05) 218

Butterstone Loch
Fly fishing for trout near Dunkeld
Daily tickets (keeper): Lochend Cottage, Butterstone Loch

Loch Faskally
Salmon plus fly fishing for fair-sized trout, NW of Pitlochry
Daily tickets: P D Malloch, 83 Atholl Road, Pitlochry
Tel: (0796) 2228

River Isla
Good trout and grayling
Free fishing beyond Airlie Castle
Further information: Tay Salmon Fisheries Board, Water Bailiff, Alyth
Tel: (082 83) 2329

Loch Kinardochy
Fly fishing only
Daily tickets: Queen's View Visitor's Centre, Allean
Tel: (079 684) 223

Loch Tay
Salmon and trout
Daily tickets in advance: W Allan, Main Street, Killin

Loch Tummel
Brown trout, perch and pike
Daily tickets in advance: Loch Tummel Hotel, Tummel Bridge

Angler's Directory for Central and South Scotland

Clubs and Associations

Annan & District Angling Club (J Trodden), 61 High Street, Annan, Dumfries and Galloway

County of Peebles Angling Improvement Association (The Secretary), 35 Edderston Road, Peebles

Dalbeattie Angling Association (G D Bomphray), 7 Urr Road, Dalbeattie, Dumfries and Galloway

Gala Angling Club (R H Watson), 41 Balmoral Avenue, Galashiels

Hawick Angling Club (R Johnston), Kelvin, 6 Raeson Park, Hawick, Borders

Jed-Forest Angling Association (J Gibson), 35 Howden Crescent, Jedburgh, Borders

Melrose and District Angling Association (The Secretary), Ravensbourne, Douglas Road, Melrose, Borders

Peeblesshire Salmon Fishing Association (Messrs Blackwood and Smith W S), 39 High Street, Peebles, Borders

Pitlochry Angling Club (c/o Pitlochry Tourist Office), 28 Atholl Road, Pitlochry, Tayside
Tel: (0796) 2215

Selkirk & District Angling Association (A Murray), 40 Raeburn Meadow, Selkirk, Borders

Stranraer & District Angling Association (J D Kinnets , Balnacoil, Largs Road, Glenluce, Dumfries and Galloway
Tel: (0776) 3312

Whiteadder Angling Association (R Welsh), Abbey Street Bathams, Duns, Borders
Tel: (036 14) 210

Tackle Shops

Annan
A Steel, 1 Murray Street
Tel: (046 12) 2365

Castle Douglas
Tommy's Sports Goods, 20 King Street

Duns
G Graham, Market Square

Kelso
T Forrest & Sons, 35 The Square

McQuillan & Wilson, High Street, Earlston
Redpath & Co, Horse Market
Tel: (057 32) 2578

Perth
B Sime, 46 South Methuen Street
Tayside Tackle, 259 High Street
Tel: (0738) 32316

Pitlochry
P D Malloch, 83 Atholl Road
Tel: (0796) 2228

Hotels and Inns

Amulree
Amulree Hotel
Tel: (035 05) 218

Dalbeattie
The Pheasant
Tel: (0556) 610345

Dunkeld
Merryburn Hotel
Tel: (035 02) 216

Duns
Cringletie House Hotel
Tel: (072 13) 233

Kelso
Ednam House Hotel
Tel: (057 32) 2168

Perth
Isle of Skye
Tel: (0738) 24471

Pitlochry
Dunalastair Hotel
Tel: (088 22) 303

Selkirk
Broadmeadows Hotel
Tel: (075 076) 227
Gordon Arms, Yarrow
Tel: (075 08) 222

North of Scotland

6

River Spey

Grantown-on-Spey – Kingussie

Angling Associations
Badenoch Angling Association
Strathspey Angling Association

Tackle shops and other ticket sources
Badenock Hotel, Newtonmore
The Boat Hotel, Boat of Garten
Craigard Hotel, Boat of Garten
Craiglyinne Hotel, Boat of Garten
W B Grant Mains of Garten Farm (Self-catering holidays)
Kelman's Stores, Boat of Garten
A Macdonald, 6 Gergask Avenue, Laggan
Nethy Bridge Hotel, Nethy Bridge
Osprey Fishing School, Aviemore Centre, Aviemore
The Paper Shop, Kingussie
The Post House Hotel, Aviemore
(Note: most hotels will only supply permits to residents)

Close Seasons
Salmon: October 1 – February 10 (note: some Association water closed until March 11 or 15), *trout:* October 7 – March 14 (note: on some Association water the trout season is considered to be the same as the salmon season), *coarse fish:* there is no recognised coarse fishing on the Spey

Bounded by four of the highest, wildest mountains in Britain and snaking its silver way through an emerald valley, is Scotland's second largest river, the Spey. Revered by lovers of salmon and whisky alike, the Spey flows for about a hundred miles from a humble source in the Monadhliath Mountains of Highland. In parts of the upper reaches it resembles a canal, until the crystal waters of a hundred hill streams swell its girth before entering Loch Insh. It is from here down to the sea below Fochabers that the salmon are found – sixty miles of fast-running, grey water, fringed by trees, and available to local and visiting fishermen.

Although the Spey has a reputation as a 'big fish' river, this is not substantiated in the record books. None of its salmon has managed to break a record, and if the size of fish everywhere continues to shrink, perhaps it never will. The Spey has an excellent run of grilse from July to early September which average about 6lb, and trout, sea trout and pike can also be found.

It goes without saying that to stand a chance of fishing this treasured river, anglers must stake their claim to a rod very early. Salmon fishing courses on private waters are run throughout February to April by the Osprey Fishing School at Aviemore (also weekly and week-end instruction throughout the year in wet and dry fly casting and spinning for game and coarse fish). This school also teaches Spey casting – a technique of switch casting which has been developed to overcome snagging on the river's many bank-side trees and bushes.

Aviemore, a custom-built sports and recreational centre, makes an excellent base for both the fisherman and his non-participating family. From here the upper reaches of the Spey can be plundered for rainbow trout and fair sea trout from late May (fishing is best in the evenings). Fly fishing for brown trout is rewarding – weights average 6–10oz with the occasional bonus of a larger specimen and, every now and again, a salmon. The main salmon run does, however, come later in the year. Casting from a boat on several nearby lochs is likely to add some pike and char to the day's catch.

Osprey also sells tackle and permits for both local waters and for Kingussie farther upstream. Noted for a sporting 18-hole golf course, breathtaking scenery and bracing air beneficial to those suffering from chest ailments, Kingussie attracts most of its compliment of annual anglers in the autumn when the trout, sea trout and to a lesser extent, the salmon, are running well. But sea trout are conversely better in the summer at the junction of the River Feshie with the Spey where waters are controlled by the Badenoch Angling Association. (Permits are obtainable at Kingussie and Newtonmore.)

The Boat of Garten (familiarly known as 'The Boat') is one of the most popular (and overcrowded) stretches on the Spey. Abernethy Angling Improvement Association water gives visitors ample opportunity for rainbows, sea trout and salmon – permits are available from Kelman's Stores – to avoid hordes of fellow-fishermen and enjoy some tranquillity, you are best advised to fish early and late in the day in summer months, especially when the river is low. Low water conditions are particularly good for sea trout and summer runs of finnock (small sea trout to a pound), which can give engrossing sport on normal trout fly tackle. Anglers set on salmon are advised to arrive a few weeks later in the autumn when the King of fish is in residence.

The Boat Hotel and Craigard Hotel can arrange permits as part of a resident's board and, like the Nethy Bridge Hotel further downstream, they run step-one instruction or refresher courses.

Commanding a plateau 700 feet above sea-level and looking out to the Cairngorms and down to the sylvan banks of the Spey, is Grantown. A favoured holiday resort in both winter and summer, Grantown is just about the last town on the middle-to-lower reaches where visitors stand a chance of sport. From here to Lochabers the Spey is almost exclusively privately-owned.

Grantown offers beautiful fly water for both pleasurable, long summer days and casting in the late evenings and on after dark for sea trout. A considerable stretch of the river here is controlled by the Strathspey Angling Associ-

Salmon fishing at Grantown-on-Spey

ation. Craiglynne Hotel also handles permits for the Spey and its turbulent tributary the Dulnain and for hill lochs in the area. Speyside is well-endowed with these stretches of still-water, where brown trout and pike fishing is either free or modestly priced (information from tackle shops in Grantown, Kingussie and Newtonmore). There is the odd pike in the Spey too, which falls to Devons and Spons meant for salmon.

As experienced Spey anglers know, casting for salmon in summer calls for light rods and low water flies. Hairwing singles, doubles and small tubes are popular: Stoat's Tail, Blue Charm, Ackroyd, Garry, Silver Doctor and Black Doctor. Natural baits: prawn, shrimp and worm are allowed on some stretches and spinning with Spey Devons (wooden or plastic), Yellow Belly, Blue and Silver, Brown and Gold and Black and Gold, is permitted in the spring. Popular flies for sea trout include Grouse and Claret, Black Spider, Peter Ross, Grouse and Green and Invicta. Fishing for salmon or sea trout is not allowed on Sundays and even chances for brown trout are severely restricted.

The dramatic countryside of this part of the Highlands abounds in outdoor activities. At Loch Morlich in the heart of the 4 000-acre Glen More Forest Park, the sandy shores are ideal for family games, picnics or sunbathing and the waters for sailing and canoeing as well as fishing. The surrounding pinewoods are latticed with short and longer treks (all are waymarked) which start at the Information Centre. To get a panoramic view of the Forest, take the two-stage ski lift from Corrie Glas to within 500 feet of the summit of Cairngorm. From here it is but a gentle walk to the top of one of Britain's highest peaks and a breathtaking vista of mountains, lochs and rivers. Only the very lucky see a red deer, a ptarmigan or a golden eagle, but a herd of imported reindeer may be observed at close quarters by joining the herdsman on his daily round of the mountains.

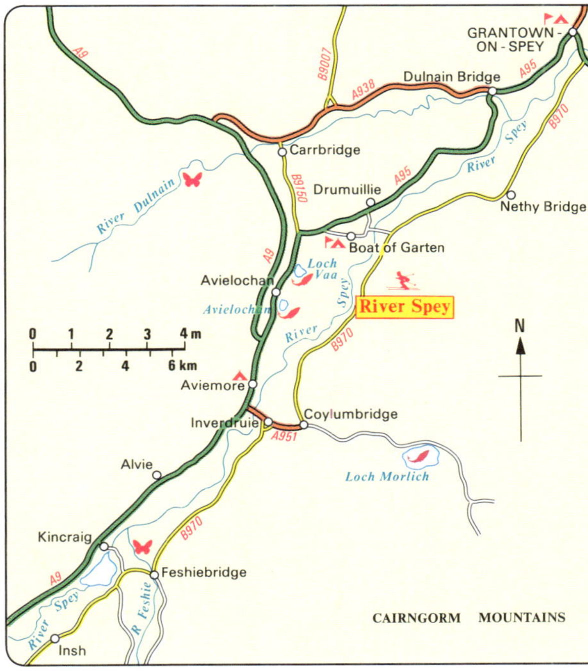

Avielochan
Trout lake SW of Boat of Garten
Daily tickets: as River Dulnain or Craigard Hotel, Boat of Garten

River Dulnain
Mainly salmon plus some trout, with good chances for the visitor
Daily tickets: G Mortimer, 61 High Street, Grantown-on-Spey
Tel: (0479) 2684

River Feshie
Meandering stream offering some access for salmon and sea trout
Daily tickets: The Paper Shop, King Street, Kingussie
Tel: (054 02) 207

Loch Morlich
Trout fishing 5m SE of Aviemore
Daily tickets (keeper): The Warden, Glenmore Forest Park

Loch Vaa
Fly fishing for reasonable trout 3m SW of Boat of Garten
Daily tickets: as Avielochan

Osprey Fishing School
Centre at Aviemore offering boat fishing on the Spey and lochs, with facilities for disabled anglers
Tel: (0479) 810767

The pure waters of the Spey and its tributaries are a vital ingredient in making Scotland's malt whiskies, and between Keith and Grantown-on-Spey several distilleries welcome visitors to a short guided tour and to sample a wee dram. Among these are Glenfarclas, Glenfiddich, Glenlivet and Tamdhu.

Just about every conceivable sport is covered at the Aviemore Centre, from curling and crazy golf to gliding and ski-ing. Craftsmen can be watched at work at the Highland Craft Centre, and clan connections (should they exist) can be traced at the Clan Tartan Centre. Kingussie's Highland Folk Museum goes a step further and illustrates just what it was like to be a Highlander in the old days. The Aviemore Centre is open all year and has a limitless range of indoor pursuits plus an additional selection of summer and snow season activities. There are fourteen pistes, all requiring varying degrees of skill, from beginners to very experienced, and no fewer than six schools to give tuition. Four chairlifts and eight ski-tows are hard at work each day ferrying skiers to the higher slopes.

Aviemore is the terminus of the Strathspey Steam Railway which chugs back and forth for five miles to Boat of Garten. Another way of sightseeing is by horseback and there are pony trekking centres at Carrbridge, Nethy Bridge, Laggan and Aviemore.

Few places in Britain can offer quite such a range of outdoor activities in such a beautiful setting. Whether the Spey valley appeals purely to the senses or to a desire for achievement, there is as much enjoyment in breathing the fresh mountain air as catching a bright silver salmon from the banks of the Spey or a trout or two from Avielochan.

Camping
Aviemore: Speyside Caravan Park ►►►
Tel: (0479) 810236
Level 104-pitch site (no tents)
Open Apr then Jun–Aug no bookings
Boat of Garten: Boat of Garten Camping & Caravanning Park ►►►
Even 50-pitch site
Open all year (ex Nov) no bookings
Grantown-on-Spey: Municipal Caravan Site ►►►
Partly sloping 360-pitch site
Open Easter–Sep, no bookings

Golfing
Boat of Garten:
Tel: (047 983) 282
Parkland course with good views, 18 holes, 5637yds, par 70, SSS68
Grantown-on-Spey:
Tel: (0479) 2079
Varied woodland course, 18 holes, 5683yds, par 70, SSS67

Riding
Grantown-on-Spey: Nethy Bridge Pony Trekking & Riding Centre, Nethy Bridge (5m SW of Grantown-on-Spey)
Tel: (047 982) 693

Ski-ing
Aviemore: Strathspey Hotel: ski instruction & equipment hire
Tel: (0479) 810681

Walking Trails
Glenmore Forest Park: many woodland walks plus various sports facilities (10m E of Aviemore)

General
Aviemore: Aviemore Centre: vast indoor leisure complex including ice rink, swimming pool, cinema, theatre
Tel: (0479) 810624
Boat of Garten: Strathspey Railway: 5m journey by steam train
Open mid-May–Sep Sat & Sun, plus Tue, Wed & Thur Jul–Aug
Carrbridge: Landmark: large tourist centre with film shows, craft displays, nature trails (7m N of Aviemore)
Open all year – 9.30–10.30 (winter 9.30–5)
Kincraig: Highland Wild Life Park: many animals including bears, bison, reindeer, wolves
Open Mar–Oct daily 10–6
Tel: (054 04) 270

Angler's Directory for the North of Scotland

Clubs and Associations

Abernethy Angling Improvement Association (J McInnes), Balnafoich, Boat of Garten, Highland
Tel: (047 983) 260

Badenoch Angling Association (Mrs J Walker), 39 Burnside Avenue, Aviemore, Highland

Strathspey Angling Improvement Association (G G Mortimer), 61 High Street, Grantown-on-Spey, Highland
Tel: (0479) 2684

Tackle Shops

Aviemore

Abu Fishing Centre

Osprey Fishing School
Tel: (0479) 810767

Grantown-on-Spey

G G Mortimer, 61 High Street
Tel: (0479) 2684

A Stuart, High Street
Tel: (0479) 2612

Kingussie

The Paper Shop (for daily tickets only), King Street
Tel: (054 02) 207

Hotels and Inns

Aviemore

Strathspey Hotel
Tel: (0479) 810681

Boat of Garten

The Boat Hotel
Tel: (047 983) 258

Grantown-on-Spey

Seafield Lodge Hotel
Tel: (0479) 2152